What readers are saying about IN 30 MINUTES® guides:

Twitter In 30 Minutes

"A perfect introduction to Twitter. Quick and easy re[...]tos. I finally understand the # symbol!"

"Clarified any issues and concerns I had and [...]llent precautions."

Genealogy Basics In 30 Minutes

"This basic genealogy book is a fast, informative read that will get you on your way if you are ready to begin your genealogy journey or are looking for tips to push past a problem area."

"The personal one-on-one feel and the obvious dedication it took to boil down a lot of research into such a small book and still make it readable are the two reasons I give this book such a high rating. Recommended."

Crowdfunding Basics In 30 Minutes

"Very understandable and absorbing. A must-read for any entrepreneur."

"On the verge of launching a crowdfunding campaign myself, this book has made me re-think my plans and my strategy. Take a step back and get the advice of someone who's been there."

LinkedIn In 30 Minutes

"This was an excellent primer for someone like me who had a LinkedIn account but didn't really use it except to look up people."

"Since reading this a week ago, I have had more quality business interactions on LinkedIn than I have had in the last 2 years."

Dropbox In 30 Minutes

"I was intimidated by the whole idea of storing my files in the cloud, but this book took me through the process and made it so easy."

"This was truly a 30-minute tutorial and I have mastered the basics without bugging my 20-year-old son! Yahoo!"

"Very engaging and witty."

*Learn more about IN 30 MINUTES® guides at **in30minutes.com***

Google Drive & Docs

In 30 Minutes

The unofficial guide to Google Drive,
Docs, Sheets & Slides

SECOND EDITION

Ian Lamont

IN 30 MINUTES® Guides

Published by i30 Media Corporation
Newton, Massachusetts

Copyright © 2015-2018
i30 Media Corporation
An *IN 30 MINUTES*® Guide
All Rights Reserved
ISBN: 978-1939924-31-5
Library of Congress Control Number: 2018936063

No part of this publication may be reproduced, distributed, or transmitted in any form or by any means, including photocopying, recording, or other electronic or mechanical methods, without the prior written permission of the publisher, except in the case of brief quotations embodied in critical reviews and certain other noncommercial uses permitted by copyright law. IN 30 MINUTES® is a trademark of i30 Media Corporation. Visit in30minutes.com for more information.

The author and the publisher make no representations with respect to the contents hereof and specifically disclaim any implied or express warranties of merchantability or fitness for any particular usage, application, or purpose. The author and the publisher cannot be held liable for any direct, indirect, incidental, consequential, or special damages of any kind, or any damages whatsoever, including, without limitation, those resulting in loss of profit, loss of contracts, goodwill, data, income, information, anticipated savings or business relationships, arising out of or in connection with the use of this book or any links within.

i30 Media Corporation and IN 30 MINUTES® guides are not associated with other brand names, product names, or trademarks cited in this book, including the Google Drive™ online storage service. *Google Drive & Docs In 30 Minutes* is an independent publication and is not affiliated with, nor has it been authorized, sponsored, or otherwise approved by Google Inc. Google and the Google logo are registered trademarks of Google Inc., used with permission. Screenshots featured in this guide are used for informational purposes, education, and commentary. Profile images and other samples are used with permission. Individual Google profiles and profile pictures are included solely for educational and demonstrative purposes. Author and publisher in no way represent that such profiles are complete, accurate, or current as reproduced or excerpted in this book.

Original interior design by Monica Thomas for TLC Graphics, www.TLCGraphics.com. Interior design assisted and composition by Rick Soldin, book-comp.com.

Contents

Why you need to use Google's free office suite

Thanks for reading *Google Drive & Docs In 30 Minutes, 2nd Edition*. I wrote this unofficial user guide to help people get up to speed with Google's remarkable (and free) online office suite that includes file storage (Google Drive), a word processor (Google Docs), a spreadsheet program (Google Sheets), and a presentation tool (Google Slides). It also includes a tool for creating online survey forms (Google Forms) and an online publishing tool (Google Sites).

How do people use these applications? There are many possible uses. Consider these examples:

➤ **Jeanette, a harried product manager for a global manufacturer, needs to work on an important proposal over the weekend.** In the past, she would have dug around in her bag to look for an old USB drive she uses for transferring files. Or, she might have emailed herself an attachment to open at home. Not anymore. Now she saves the Word document and an Excel spreadsheet to Google Drive at the office. Later that evening, on her home PC, she opens her Google Drive folder to access and edit the files. All of her saves are updated to Google Drive. When she returns to work the following Monday, the updated data can be viewed at her workstation.

➤ **Graham is organizing a family reunion and wants to survey 34 cousins** about attendance, lodging preferences, and potluck dinner preparation (always a challenge—the Nebraska branch of the family won't eat corn or Garbanzo beans). He emails everyone a link to an online form he created using Google Forms. Relatives open the form on their browsers or phones, and submit their answers. The answers are automatically transferred to Google Sheets, where Graham can view the responses and sort the results.

➤ A small business consultant named Charlotte is helping the owner of Slappy's Canadian Diner ("*We Put the Canadian Back in Bacon!*") **prepare a slideshow for potential franchisees in Ohio.** She and Slappy, who is based in Vancouver, collaborate using Google Slides. Charlotte shares a link to the slideshow with her consulting partner Lauren, so she can periodically review it on the Google Slides app on her phone and check for problems. Each collaborator can remotely access the deck and add text, images, and other elements, even if someone else is making revisions at the same time! Later, Slappy meets his potential franchise operators at a hotel in Cleveland, and uses Google Slides on his iPad to pitch his business.

➤ **An elementary school faculty uses Docs to collaborate on lesson plans.** Each teacher accesses the same document from home or the classroom. Updates are instantly reflected in the document, even when two teachers are simultaneously accessing it. Public-facing documents for parents and educational YouTube videos are published on Google Sites. Their principal (known as "Skinner" behind his back) is impressed by how quickly the faculty completes the plans, and how well the curriculums are integrated.

➤ At the same school, **5th-grade teacher Nick Lee asks students to submit homework using Docs.** Nick adds corrections and notes, which the students can access at home using a web browser. It's much more efficient than emailing attachments, and the students don't need to bug their parents to purchase Microsoft Office.

Many people are introduced to Google's online office suite through Docs, the popular online word processor. Others are attracted by the free storage and syncing features of Google Drive. A subscription to Office 365, which includes Word, Excel, PowerPoint, OneDrive, and other Microsoft software, can cost more than one hundred dollars per year. While Drive and the other Google applications are not as sophisticated as Microsoft Office, they handle basic documents and spreadsheets very well. The suite also offers a slew of powerful online features, including:

➤ The ability to review the history of a specific document, and revert to an earlier version.

➤ Simple web forms and online surveys which can be produced without programming skills or website hosting arrangements.

➤ Collaboration features that let users work on the same document in real time.

➤ Offline file storage that can be synced to multiple computers.

➤ Automatic notification of the release date of Brad Pitt's next movie.

I'm just kidding about the last item. But Google Drive, Docs, Sheets, Forms, Slides, and Sites really can do those other things—and without the help of your company's IT department or the pimply teenager from down the street. The features are built right into the software, and are ready to use as soon as you've signed up.

Even though the myriad features of Google's office suite may seem overwhelming, this guide makes it easy to get started. *Google Drive & Docs In 30 Minutes* is written in plain English, with lots of step-by-step instructions, screenshots, and tips. More resources are available on the companion website to this book, *googledrive.in30minutes.com*. You'll get up to speed in no time.

This edition of *Google Drive & Docs In 30 Minutes* covers interface improvements that Google has rolled out in recent years, as well as the expanded capabilities of the Google Drive, Docs, Sheets, and Slides apps for iOS and Android. It also contains basic instructions for the new Google Forms and Google Sites. Please note that Google is constantly updating the applications and the software interfaces, so don't be surprised if some features work a little differently than described in this guide.

We've only got 30 minutes, so let's get started. If you are using a PC or laptop, please download the Google Chrome browser, which works best with Google's web applications. Instructions for the mobile apps are referenced throughout the guide.

CHAPTER 1

Getting started with Drive and Google's mobile apps

It takes seconds to set up Google Drive, Docs, Sheets, Slides, Drawings, Forms, and Sites. The registration requirements are startlingly simple. All you need to do is provide an email address and answer a few basic questions on a web form or on your phone. No discs or downloads are needed!

This chapter will also explain the Google Drive interface, and will give some tips on how to organize your files and folders. For this and all other chapters, I recommend using the Google Chrome browser, which is available for Windows, Macs, and Linux desktop and laptop computers, as well as Chromebook notebooks. If you don't have it installed, visit *chrome.google. com* for instructions to download and install the browser.

Before we get started, I have a quick note relating to nomenclature.

What's the difference between Google Drive and Google Docs?

Google has struggled with branding its online office suite, and some confusion may linger concerning which app does what. Here is a quick list of the applications and basic functionality:

➤ **Google Drive is used for storage of files,** including non-Google formats such as Microsoft Office documents. It also has a folder/file hierarchy used to view and access files. It's similar to OneDrive and Dropbox.

➤ **Google Docs is the online word processor.** Docs has similar functionality to Microsoft Word.

➤ **Google Sheets is the online spreadsheet program,** similar to Microsoft Excel.

➤ **Google Slides is the presentation program,** similar to Microsoft PowerPoint.

➤ **Google Forms** lets users create online forms for data entry, such as a survey or sign-up sheet. Data entered into Google Forms will appear in an associated Google Sheets file.

➤ **Google Drawings** can be used to draw shapes, text, and other elements for basic illustrations or annotated photos.

➤ **Google Sites** is an online publishing tool, closely integrated with Google Drive and other Google services.

➤ **G Suite** (formerly known as Google Apps) is a collection of online services that includes all of the above programs along with other Google services not covered in this guide, such as Google Calendar. It is further branded by industry, such as G Suite for Education, G Suite for Business, and G Suite for Government.

If you are using a browser, all of these applications can be accessed via Google Drive (*drive.google.com*). On mobile devices, the standalone apps for Docs, Sheets, and Slides can be used to directly access or create documents, spreadsheets, or presentations.

Because Drive plays such a central role when it comes to organizing files, many of the instructions in this guide will refer to Drive even if it's possible to carry out the same task in Docs, Sheets, or Slides. In addition, I will sometimes use the term *Google files* as a catch-all term for documents and other content created in Google Docs, Sheets, Slides, Drawings, Forms, and Sites.

Registration

Google Drive requires a Google Account, which will let you log in to any Google service, including Drive, Gmail, YouTube, and the Android mobile operating system. Registration can be completed on a PC, laptop, or mobile device. Instructions are given below.

Some readers may also want to access the Google applications using a Chromebook, a stripped-down laptop designed to run the Google applications. Chromebooks require a Google Account to activate, so once you are logged in you can start using the applications right away.

If you already have a Gmail account or an Android phone, there is no need to create a new account. Simply use the same login credentials on *drive.google. com* or the Google Drive, Docs, Sheets, and Slides apps. More information about using the apps is given later in this chapter.

How to activate a new Google Account on a PC, Mac, or Chromebook

Here are the steps to register for Google Drive:

1. Go to *drive.google.com*. If you are not already logged in, you will be prompted to do so.

2. If you already have a Google Account, enter your Google username (the email address associated with the account) and password, and select *Sign In*. You can then skip ahead to the next section in this guide.

3. If you don't have an account, select *More options > Create an account* near the bottom of the screen.

4. You'll be prompted to submit a variety of information to create a new Google Account.

5. Enter a first and last name. Note that the name you enter will be associated with any content you create or share on any Google services, including YouTube videos, app and product reviews on Google Play, and shared Google Drive folders and files.

6. In the next field, type a username that will become your new Gmail address. Or, select *I prefer to use my current email address* and enter an existing email address that you want to associate with Google Drive and other Google services. It can be any working email address, including Yahoo Mail, a school email address, or your work email. If the username is already registered, you will be asked to create a new one.

7. Enter a password (minimum of 8 characters long).

8. Enter your birthday.

9. Enter your gender. This is mandatory, although if you are uncomfortable with this step, you can choose *Other* or *Rather not say*.

10. *Mobile Phone* is an optional field. I recommend entering a real mobile number here, as this can help prevent other people from taking control of your account—Google will use the number to verify you are the actual owner in case someone attempts to log in to Google Drive from a new computer.

11. Answer the security question to prove to Google that you are human (this helps prevent malicious computer programs from signing up for Google services and spreading spam).

12. Select your location.

13. Agree to Google's Privacy Policy and Terms of Service, and select the *Next Step* button.

14. If you've done everything right, you'll be taken to a confirmation page.

15. Check your inbox for the confirmation message that Google sent you, and follow the link to activate your Google Account. You must do this to use Google Drive and related Google applications.

16. Return to *drive.google.com*, and log on with your email address and the password you created.

17. To log out of Google Drive, click on your profile photo in the upper right corner of the browser window and press the *Sign Out* button.

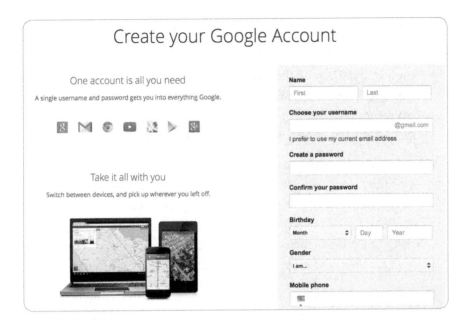

If you are using an Android phone or tablet, an iPhone, or an iPad, you will need to first download the Google Drive app via *Google Play* (Android) or the *App Store* (iOS).

Why you should use Google's mobile apps

Who would have thought that having access to your Google files on the go could be so much fun?

For some, this may seem bizarre. Indeed, I can confirm it's pure torture trying to draft a letter or enter data into a spreadsheet on a tiny phone screen while seated on a bucking subway train. The mobile formatting options in the Android and iOS apps for Docs, Sheets, and Slides are limited. In addition, many users have reported lag when entering text and performing other functions.

But other features of the Google Drive mobile app—as well as the individual apps for Google Docs, Google Sheets, and Google Slides—are quite useful. For people who don't own a laptop or PC, the mobile apps may be the only available options.

Here's what you can do with the Google Drive app as well as the individual apps for Docs, Sheets, and Slides:

➤ **Review existing documents, spreadsheets, presentations and drawings.** This is helpful if you need to review a document on the way to a meeting, and don't have time to take out your laptop. Files can be opened or previewed from the Google Drive app.

➤ **Create new documents and edit existing ones.** The latest crop of apps from Google lets users edit documents. While this is convenient for creating new documents and making simple changes, it's not possible to do serious text entry or editing unless you are using a larger tablet or an attached keyboard. On small-screen devices, text formatting is limited, and many advanced features cannot be accessed.

➤ **Turn your phone's camera into a portable scanner.** Google Drive for Android can instantly create PDFs using the camera on your phone or tablet, and save them to your Google Drive account. It's a great way to make quick records of important documents.

➤ **Upload photos and other files to your Google Drive account.** The app can import photos and other files on your device into your Google Drive account. It can also upload files from Dropbox, if the Dropbox app is installed on the same device.

➤ **Share documents with other people**. This is a perfect feature to activate after a meeting, meal, or phone call. After discussing a file on your phone or tablet, you can immediately share it using the apps for Google Docs, Google Sheets, and Google Slides.

The mobile apps share some similarities with their web counterparts. For instance, the interface for the Google Drive app on the iPad uses familiar icons:

There are many more possibilities, which are described below.

What the different apps do

Google offers the following individual apps for Android and iOS phones and tablets. Key features are listed for each app.

Google Drive

The Drive app lets users:

> ➤ Preview files, including PDF, Microsoft Office, and image files.

> ➤ Upload files stored in the mobile device, including images and videos.

> ➤ Scan documents using the device's camera (Android only). The images are automatically turned into PDFs, which are then stored in *My Drive*.

> ➤ Organize files and folders.

Google Docs

This app can be used for:

➤ Editing Microsoft Word and Google Docs documents, including typing and deleting text and applying basic formatting (text size, fonts, colors, etc.).

➤ Sharing documents with other users.

➤ Inserting images, tables, and comments.

➤ Printing documents over a wireless network (see below).

Google Sheets

The Google Sheets app lets users handle the following tasks:

➤ Opening and editing spreadsheets created in Google Sheets or Microsoft Excel.

➤ Creating and editing formulas.

➤ Applying limited formatting (fonts, background colors, borders, justification, number formats, etc.).

It's possible to view charts in the Sheets app, but chart creation is not supported.

Google Slides

The Google Slides mobile app has a limited feature set:

➤ Editing text in PowerPoint or Slides presentations.

➤ Previewing presentations.

➤ Reviewing and editing speaker notes.

➤ Adding new slides.

➤ Adding images, shapes, and text boxes.

It's not yet possible to insert or edit animations or other more sophisticated formatting and features.

Sharing and printing

Docs, Sheets, and Slides allow users to share files or links to files with other Google accounts. Printing from a mobile device can be done through Google Cloud Printing but setup is required (see the section about printing later in this chapter).

Installing apps on Android and iOS

Accessing Drive, Docs, Sheets, and Slides on a phone or tablet involves downloading the relevant apps and then activating them. If you haven't already done so, it will be necessary to create a Google Account in order to use Drive or any of the productivity apps. Note that the apps only work on Android devices and Apple products that use the iOS operating system, such as the iPhone and iPad.

Other mobile phones cannot install native Google apps for Drive, Docs, Sheets, and Slides. However, it is still possible to access Google Drive via a mobile web browser on practically any device. The mobile web option (*http://m.google.com*) gives users limited viewing, editing, and printing capabilities.

Android

Because the Android mobile operating system is a Google product, and Drive, Docs, Sheets, and Slides are also Google products, it's very easy to get the apps up and running on practically any Android phone or tablet. Some phones and tablets may already have the apps installed.

If you can't find Drive on your Android device, open *Google Play* and download Drive, followed by Docs, Sheets, and Slides.

When opened for the first time, the apps should automatically detect your Google account, either through the account you use on Google Play or the Gmail app. To add another Google account, tap the menu button or your account icon in the upper left corner of the screen and tap *Add account*.

The individual apps are small and quick to download and install.

iOS

Installing the apps for Google Drive, Docs, Slides, and Sheets on an iPhone or iPad requires a visit to the App Store. You will need to provide existing Google credentials to use the apps, or you can follow the steps described in the Registration section earlier in this chapter to create a new account.

When you open the app, you will be prompted to enter the login credentials for an existing account, or to create a new account. After logging into Drive, the iOS device will save your credentials for Docs, Sheets, and Slides.

You can also use multiple Google Accounts on a single device. Tap the Menu icon (three horizontal lines) to display the account being used (see screenshot), and then tap the tiny triangle icon and then select *Manage accounts*.

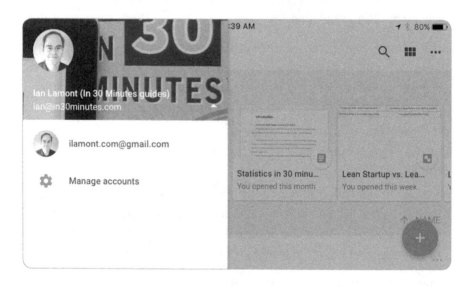

There are several very useful features in the iOS versions of these Google apps:

➤ **Offline editing.** Edit recent documents without an Internet connection.

➤ **Collaborative editing.** People can simultaneously edit a document.

➤ **Edit Microsoft Office documents.** This feature lets users make edits to existing Word, Excel, and PowerPoint files.

Navigating the main screen in Google Drive

When you log onto Google Drive for the first time on a PC, laptop, or Chromebook, you'll see something like this:

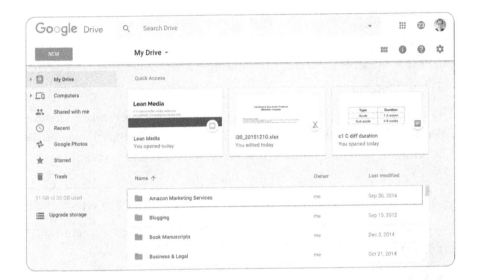

There are many elements on the screen, but here are the ones you really need to pay attention to:

New button

The *New* button is where most of the action in Drive takes place. The button is similar to the *New* menu option in many desktop software applications to create a new file. Pressing *New* will display options for creating the following types of files and folders:

> ➤ **Google Docs.** Select this option to create a new document.

> ➤ **Google Sheets.** Creates a new spreadsheet.

> ➤ **Google Slides.** Creates a new presentation.

> ➤ **More.** Options include creating a new online form in Google Forms, a drawing in Google Drawings, or a website in Google Sites.

The *New* button also has options for creating a new folder (for instance, "History Class" or "West Coast Sales Plan") as well as options for uploading files and folders.

My Drive

My Drive displays the folders in your Drive account on the left side of the browser screen. Click the small triangle next to *My Drive* to expand or collapse the list.

The list of files and folders takes up the central area of the browser window. Select a folder to see the files it contains. When you first start using Google Drive, the list will seem short. Trust me: It won't stay that way for long!

Shared, Photos, Recent, Starred and Trash

Below *My Drive* on the left side of the browser window are additional groups of files and folders:

➤ *Computers* shows devices and uploaded files and folders using Google applications such as Backup & Sync (see Chapter 7).

➤ *Shared with me* includes shared files and folders (learn more about sharing and collaboration in Chapter 6).

➤ *Google Photos* is an online photo storage service (activation required).

➤ *Recent* is a reverse-chronological list of files that you have created, uploaded, or edited.

➤ *Starred* consists of files that you have marked with a star (to do this, select the file on the Google Drive main screen, select the *More Actions* icon, and then select *Add star*).

➤ *Trash* holds deleted items in temporary storage until you permanently delete them or restore them (useful in case you change your mind). To get rid of an item for good, select it and click the *Delete forever* link at the top of the list.

Special options for selected files and folders

There are several icons that appear at the top of the Drive window *after* you
select a folder or file name:

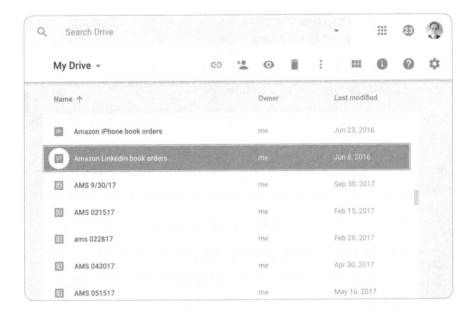

Here's what the icons do:

Get link. The chain icon lets you copy the link of the selected file. However,
unless the file is public (see *How to enable public editing* in Chapter 6),
the link can only be used by people who have sharing rights for the file in
question.

Share. The silhouette icon lets you share selected files or folders. Click the
icon, enter an email address, and select the level of sharing. A more detailed
explanation about sharing files and folders can be found in Chapter 6.

Preview. The eye icon lets you preview a file, with the option of opening it
in the corresponding Google application.

Trash icon. This icon makes it easy to *remove* files. Just press the garbage
can, and the selected items will be put in the holding pen for Trash. Permanently deleting the files requires an extra step, as described earlier.

More Actions. The three dots icon expands a new menu with options to open files or folders, create new folders, add stars, rename the selected file or folder, view details about the selected file or folder, or download the file or folder contents to your hard drive.

Grid view/list view. This button toggles the view of files and folders, using large icons or a list of the contents.

View details. The "i" icon shows information about a file or folder, including the date of creation and its location.

Settings. The gear icon accesses Google Drive's settings, described later in this guide.

Once you are comfortable with Google Drive's main screen and some of the basic commands, you can refer to the glossary of keyboard shortcuts at the back of this guide to quickly navigate the screen and activate basic features.

Preview mode

Clicking or tapping certain types of files in My Drive will open them in Preview mode. Here's an example of a .csv (comma-separated values) file being previewed in a browser window. The file cannot be edited, but the basic contents are visible:

The toolbar is a quick way to print, download, share, or open the file for editing or conversion. Functions include:

Open with. Select a Google application or third-party app to open a file (see Chapter 5 for more information about installing third-party apps).

Print. Sends the file to the local or network printer. Certain previewed documents can also be saved as PDFs.

Download. The down arrow downloads a copy of the file to the designated Downloads folder on your hard drive.

More Actions. Clicking the three dots lets you share, move, rename, see details, or "star" the document (i.e., mark the file for future reference or follow-up).

Zoom. Examine the file close up, to better see certain details.

Note that native Google Docs, Sheets, and Slides files won't preview in a browser—they will simply open in the relevant Google application. However, in the Google Drive mobile app, Preview mode extends to Google Docs, Sheets, and Slides files. To edit them, tap the pencil icon at the top of the screen.

Organizing Google Drive

You're going to use Google Drive a lot. Over the course of a year, scores of letters, reports, spreadsheets, shared folders with other people (more on that in Chapter 6), and other types of files will end up in your Google Drive account. Using the apps within Google Drive, you can create as many documents, spreadsheets and presentations as you want. For non-Google formats such as Microsoft Word documents or .jpg images, there is a cap (currently 15 gigabytes, but I expect this to rise) that comes with your Google Account.

It can be tricky finding a specific file once you have hundreds listed on your Google Drive homepage. The following section will describe some steps you can take to tame the clutter.

How to use search in Google Drive

The search field is located at the top of the browser window. It lets you search the contents of every file in your Google Drive repository. It may not seem important now, but once you have a lot of files in Drive, you'll find yourself using search all the time.

Here's what you need to know about search in Drive:

➤ **You can search for the file name** ("Christmas wish list"), or a **portion of the file name** ("wish").

➤ **You can search for text or keywords** that appear in the body of a document, spreadsheet, or presentation.

➤ **Search by file type** (for example, only PDFs).

How to use folders

While search in Google Drive is effective, it doesn't work so well when you have lots of files or need to collaborate with people on groups of files. For these reasons, I recommend creating folders in Google Drive. Folders are easy to set up:

1. Press the *New* button and select *Folder*.

2. Name the folder and press *Create*.

3. On Google Drive's main page, drag files to the folder you just created.

It's also possible to create subfolders within a Google Drive folder. In addition, if you already have folders on your desktop or laptop, you can upload them using the *New* button.

An alternate way of managing your Google Drive files and folders is to use the Google Drive desktop application (see Chapter 7, *How to add files to Google Drive using a PC or Mac*).

Printing

Printing a document, spreadsheet, presentation, or drawing is straightforward—in most cases, it's simply a matter of clicking the Print icon.

However, setting up printers can be tricky, particularly when wireless printers are involved.

Printing with a wired printer

If you are using a home or office printer connected to a PC or laptop with a USB cable, printing is easy:

1. Open the document in the Google Chrome browser.
2. Make sure the printer is turned on, loaded with paper, and no other jobs are in the queue.
3. Click the print icon and follow the instructions.

Not all Chromebooks have direct printing functionality—you'll need to set up Google Cloud Print (see below).

Google Cloud Print and wireless printers

If you have access to a wireless-enabled printer, you can print Google Docs, Sheets, and Slides documents from PCs, laptops, Chromebooks, and mobile devices. This is possible using Google Cloud Print, which connects devices to printers via Wi-Fi networks.

Unfortunately, in practice, I have found Google Cloud Print to be hard to configure, particularly when using browsers other than Chrome. Sometimes the only option is to download a PDF, and then print that from another application (such as Adobe Acrobat or macOS Preview).

Here are some other considerations when using Google Cloud Print:

➤ Google Cloud Print requires extra installation steps using a "Cloud Ready" printer.

➤ Google Cloud Print services are associated with individual Google accounts. If you have multiple Google accounts, make sure that you use the same account when you are attempting to print.

Google advises owners of Cloud Ready printers to first follow the manufacturers' instructions relating to connecting the printer to your local Wi-Fi network. Then, follow these steps:

PCs and laptops

1. Once the printer has been connected to the network, it should appear as an available printing option when using Google Docs, Sheets, or Slides in the Google Chrome browser.

2. If not, use Chrome to visit *http://www.google.com/cloudprint/learn/* and click the *Go to my Cloud Print* button.

3. Select the *Add Cloud Ready Printer* link, and follow the instructions for your printer.

4. When trying to print a document using Google Cloud Print, you may see options to "print" to Google Drive, commercial services, and other mobile devices. These are used for remote printing or sending PDF files.

Android phones and tablets

1. Google Cloud Print services may already be enabled. To check, open the Google Docs app, select a file, and then *Share & export > Print*. If you see the wireless printer in the list, you can start printing.

2. If not, open the Google Play app store and find the Google Cloud Print app. Install it.

3. Go to the menu (the three bars icon) and select *Add printers*. If the printer has already been added to another computer or device on the network, it may not be visible, but it should still be available for the next step.

4. When using *Share & export > Print* in the Google Docs, Sheets, and Slides apps, available Cloud Ready printers will be displayed.

IOS phones and tablets

Google Cloud Print services should be visible when opening a document in Google Docs.

1. Press the More Actions icon (three dots).

2. Select *Print preview*, and then press More Actions again.

3. Select *Print*, and then choose *Cloud Print* or *AirPrint* (Apple's wireless printing technology).

Other Google files can be printed directly from the Google Drive app for iOS.

1. Press the More Actions icon (three dots).

2. Scroll down and tap *Print*.

3. Select *Cloud Print* or *AirPrint*.

If you do not see a Cloud Ready printer that has already been configured, make sure you are logged into the same Google account that you used to add the printer to the network.

Working with Microsoft Office formats

Google knows that most of its users work with Microsoft Office files. Even if you don't have Microsoft Office installed, colleagues or classmates may email you Office attachments, or they may insist you send them Office attachments because they don't use Google's online office suite.

Google has made it relatively easy to convert files between Microsoft Office and Google Docs, Sheets, and Slides. In addition, Google has added functionality to its mobile apps, Chromebooks, and the Google Chrome web browser that lets users edit the original Word, Excel, and PowerPoint files.

Direct editing of Microsoft Office formats

Users can edit Microsoft Word, Excel, and PowerPoint files in Google Docs, Sheets, and Slides using Office Compatibility Mode. This feature comes built into Chromebooks and the mobile apps for Android and iOS, and can be activated on the Chrome browser on PCs and Macs (go to *Window > Extensions*, search for *Office Editing for Docs, Sheets & Slides* and install).

However, there are some limitations:

➤ Formatting and image placement may look different when Microsoft Office files are opened in Office Compatibility Mode.

➤ Office Compatibility Mode will not work with Internet Explorer, Firefox, Safari, or other browsers.

➤ Files with the .doc, .docx, .xls, .xlsx, .ppt, and .pptx extensions can be edited if they were created in Microsoft Office 2007 or newer versions of Microsoft Office. Older files (created in Microsoft Office 2003 and earlier) are not supported unless they are resaved with a more recent version of Microsoft Office.

➤ It may not be possible to edit certain files, such as large Excel spreadsheets.

Protip: Collaborative editing (described in Chapter 6, *Collaboration*) is not possible when Microsoft Office files are opened for editing. However, it is possible to convert Office files to the equivalent Google formats for collaborative editing.

Converting Microsoft Office formats to Google formats

When you upload a Word document (files ending with .doc or .docx), Excel spreadsheet (.xls, .xlsx), or PowerPoint presentation (.ppt, .pptx) to Google Drive, you have the option of converting them to the equivalent formats in Google Docs, Sheets, and Slides.

Converting these formats not only lets you edit them in Docs/Sheets/Slides, but also lets you collaborate on them with other people (see Chapter 6).

There are some drawbacks, however:

➤ Microsoft formatting may be stripped out or replaced with formatting elements that look quite different in Google applications. This is not much of an issue for a simple report or spreadsheet, but it can be a big problem for brochures, presentations, and other files that have sophisticated formatting.

➤ Some features available in Microsoft Office are not available in the equivalent Google format, or are implemented much differently. Examples include *Track changes*, comments, and master slides.

➤ If the file needs to be brought back into Microsoft Office, another conversion process will have to take place.

Conversion can take place automatically during the upload process. Alternatively, you can select the uploaded file in Drive and use one of the following methods to convert it:

➤ Right-click over the selected file and choose *Open with*.

➤ Click the More Actions icon (three dots) at the top of the screen and select the option to open it in Google Docs/Sheets/Slides.

➤ Preview the file, then select the *Open with* option.

CHAPTER 2

Google Docs

Google's suite of apps has many uses. However, if I had to name the killer features, they would be the ability to instantly create or edit online documents, spreadsheets, presentations, and other types of files from any web browser or Chromebook, or the free apps for Android and iOS phones and tablets. They are a cheap, quick and effective substitute for Microsoft Office.

This chapter will explain how to get started with Docs, the most popular application in the suite after Google Drive. Docs is also the easiest to get started with. Go to *docs.google.com* to begin, or download the Google Docs app for Android and iOS.

Please also refer to the book's website (*googledrive.in30minutes.com*) for additional resources. The site includes a FAQ, as well as short videos to help you get up to speed with creating documents and other files.

Docs basics

Docs was launched in 2006. At the time, there were no other programs in the suite. It's still the most popular standalone application—everyone needs a word processor for business, school, or personal use. It's more than adequate for performing the following tasks:

➤ Composing a letter (see screenshot, below).

➤ Writing a speech.

➤ Building a report with graphics and a table of contents.

➤ Preparing an itinerary or event schedule.

➤ Building a résumé.

➤ Creating a flyer or simple sign.

➤ Exporting PDFs.

➤ Printing.

Is Docs suitable for creating more complex documents, such as a doctoral dissertation or a slick newsletter? The answer to both questions is no. You'll still need to use Microsoft Word or professional-grade publishing tools for heavy-duty formatting or footnoting.

But for other tasks, Docs does the job. Further, it offers features that haven't yet been introduced to Microsoft Office, such as Explore, Drawings, and Add-ons. I use Docs to write reports and letters and rely heavily upon the collaboration features (see Chapter 6) when I am preparing new *In 30 Minutes* guides for publication.

In this section, I'll cover the basics. They include:

➤ Creating, naming, and saving files (these instructions apply to other Google applications, including Sheets, Slides, Forms, Drawings, and Sites).

➤ Applying simple formatting changes.

➤ Exporting and printing.

Once you are comfortable with the basic commands, you may want to refer to the helpful glossary of keyboard shortcuts in the back of this guide.

Navigating Google Docs (browser/Chromebook)

It's possible to open an existing Google Docs file directly from Google Drive. However, it's also possible to open a file from the Google Docs home screen, which is distinct from Google Drive's main screen.

This is what the Google Docs home screen looks like in a web browser or Chromebook:

Here's what the icons do:

Menu. The icon that looks like three bars lets you switch to Drive, Sheets, or Slides, or access *Settings*, which includes *Offline editing* (see Chapter 7, *Working offline*).

List View/Grid View. Switches between thumbnails of the Google Docs and Word documents stored in your account, and a list view that shows the titles.

AZ button. Changes how the view is sorted (for instance, *By title* or *Last modified*).

Open File Picker. The folder icon lets users search for documents, and upload new documents.

Plus icon. This large icon on the bottom of the screen creates a new Google Docs document.

Next to each document, you will also notice an icon that looks like three dots. This is the *More Actions icon*, which displays the following functions:

➤ *Rename*

➤ *Remove*

➤ *Open in new tab*

Navigating Google Docs (Android/iOS)

The Google Docs mobile app looks a lot like the browser application, including having a plus icon to create new files (see screenshot, below). The Menu icon (three bars) has additional functions:

➤ *Recent*—Recently opened or uploaded documents.

➤ *Shared with me*—These documents have been created by other Google users and shared with you. If it's empty, it means no one has shared documents with you (yet).

➤ *Starred*—These are documents that you have "starred" for future reference or follow-up.

➤ *Offline*—Documents which are saved locally, and are therefore accessible for offline editing (see Chapter 7)

➤ *Settings*—Switch accounts, set a passcode, and change notification preferences.

➤ *Notifications*—Alerts for shared files.

Note that the Android version may have a few more features, but the basic writing and organizational tools are practically identical.

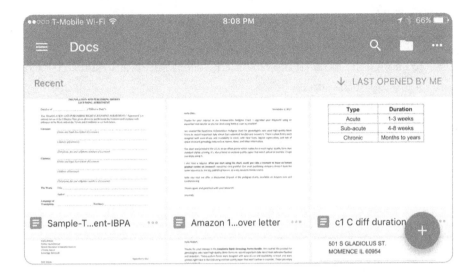

The More Actions icon below each document in the Google Docs mobile app has additional functionality:

➤ Add people

➤ Get link

➤ Send a copy

➤ Save as Word (.docx)

➤ Make a copy

➤ Move

➤ Available offline

➤ Star

➤ Rename

➤ Remove

➤ Print

How to create a new document in Docs
Browser/Chromebook

1. Open *drive.google.com* and log on.

2. From the Google Drive main screen: Click the *New* button on the left side of the screen. You will see different formats to choose from. Pick *Google Docs.*

3. From the Google Docs main screen: Click the plus icon.

4. A blank document will appear (see screenshot, below). You can start typing right away.

5. To change the name of the document, select the default "untitled" text at the top of the screen.

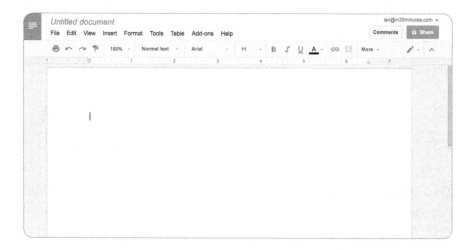

The document is now ready for you to add text, pictures and other elements. You can type some text to get started. There is no "save" function—Docs auto-saves as you type.

To close the document and return to the Google Docs home screen, select the blue icon with white lines in the upper left corner.

Android/iOS

1. Open the Google Docs app.

2. Tap the large plus icon.

3. Enter a name for the document.

Tap the pencil icon to enter text or add other elements to the file. To close the document and return to the Google Docs home screen, tap the arrow in the upper left corner of the screen.

How to rename a document
Browser/Chromebook

To rename a document while it's open, simply double-click the existing title, and enter a new name.

A document can also be renamed by selecting the More Actions icon from the Google Docs home screen, or by selecting the file in Google Drive and then selecting the More Actions icon, or right-clicking and selecting *Rename*.

Android/iOS

From the Google Docs home screen, tap the More Actions icon next to the file in question, and select *Rename*.

How to format a document

The following section covers formatting for Google Docs in a browser or Chromebook. Because formatting options in the Google Docs mobile apps are very limited, I advise switching to a desktop browser or Chromebook to format a document.

If you've used Microsoft Word or formatted email with Outlook or a web-based email program such as Yahoo Mail or Gmail, most of the menu selections and buttons in the Docs toolbar (shown below) will look familiar:

The Print icon should be self-explanatory. Other toolbar formatting buttons include:

➤ **Paragraph styles.** Besides *Normal Text*, a limited number of heading styles are available.

➤ **Fonts.** You can choose from several dozen serif, sans-serif, and special fonts and change the size.

➤ **Font decoration.** Bold/underline/italics can be activated with buttons, as well as text color (the underlined letter *A*) and background color.

➤ **Text alignment.** Indentation, centered text, flush right.

➤ **Internal/External Links.** The chain icon lets you add URLs to selected text, as well as links to internal bookmarks (which can be placed using the *Insert > Bookmark* command).

Additional formatting options are available via the *Format* menu.

Inserting images, page numbers, and more

The *Insert* command on the browser-based version of Google Docs is an easy way to import various graphics, text and other objects, including:

➤ **Images.** Upload a photo, drag a photo, reference a photo's URL, or even take a photo with a webcam. Once the image is inserted, select it to show the text-wrapping options.

➤ **Drawings.** Selecting this brings up the Google Drawings application (see Chapter 5), and lets you make quick diagrams.

➤ **Charts.** Insert basic pie, line, and bar charts. Edit chart data in Google Sheets.

➤ **Footnotes.** These are automatically numbered at the bottom of the page.

➤ **Special characters.** The list includes math symbols, arrows, non-Roman scripts, and even game pieces.

➤ **Headers and page numbers.** Unlike Microsoft Word, which allows the creation of sophisticated graphics and other header/footer elements, Google Docs only has simple text and formatting options for headers and page numbers. However, it is possible to insert a graphic logo in the header.

➤ **Table of Contents.** This function lets users create a simple TOC based on headings in the body of the document.

➤ **Comments.** Comments appear in the right margin, and are color-coded if collaborators have access.

Note that the *Insert* options in the Google Docs app for iOS and Android are limited.

Import and export options

Heavy users of Google Docs frequently have to import Microsoft Word documents, or export Word and PDF files. There are additional conversion features supported by Google Docs.

Exporting Word, PDF, and text formats

Docs auto-saves what you are doing as you type. There are other options to save, download, and export your file, using the *File* menu:

➤ **Rename.** Select *File > Rename*, or select the title at the top of the browser window and retype the new name over the existing name.

➤ **Make a copy.** This creates an identical version of the Google Docs file, and prompts you to give it a new name.

➤ **Download as.** This is an export function and lets users save documents as:

▷ **Microsoft Word** (.docx).

▷ **OpenDocument** (.odt).

▷ **Text and Rich Text** (.txt and .rtf).

▷ **PDF.** Note that on-screen formatting in Google Docs does not always match what comes out in the PDF, but for basic letters, résumés, and reports, it's usually a close match.

▷ **Web page.** Docs will save your file as an HTML document.

▷ **EPUB.** This format is used for the creation of ebooks.

In the Google Docs app for Android and iOS, export options are hidden under the More Actions icon (three dots) in an open document. Select *Share & Export* to access the following options:

➤ **Add people.** Enable collaboration or view-only sharing.

➤ **Send a copy.** Create a PDF or Word version of the document to transfer via email, Bluetooth, etc.

➤ **Print.** Send the document to a printer. Note that printing a paper copy of the document requires configuring Google Cloud Print beforehand.

➤ **Save as Word.** Saves a .docx version of the current document.

➤ **Make a copy.** Duplicates the document, and prompts you to rename the new version.

➤ **Copy link to clipboard.** Copies a link to the web version of the document, which can then be pasted into emails, a browser, or other files.

How to import documents from other programs

Google Drive and Docs can import and convert all kinds of files. Compatibility may be limited, however. This is especially true of .doc or .docx files that were heavily formatted in Microsoft Word, as well as heavily formatted .rtf files. If the formatting is not supported in Docs, it will be changed or stripped out.

Below this paragraph, the image on the top is an actual .docx file, made with a Microsoft Word newsletter template. The image on the bottom is the same file after it was imported into Google Drive and converted into a Docs file. As you can see, the headers and images were stripped out and the fonts don't match up:

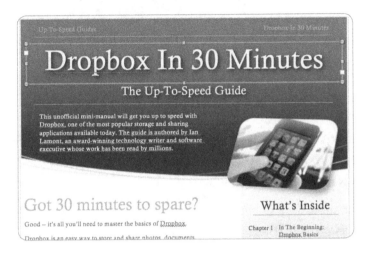

Conversion issues are less likely to occur for simple reports, letters, and résumés which are not heavily formatted.

Uploaded Microsoft Word .doc or .docx files may be automatically converted to Google Docs editor format, but conversion can be disabled in the settings for Google Drive. To convert a Microsoft Word document to Google Docs after it's been uploaded, refer to the instructions in Chapter 1, *Working with Microsoft Office formats.*

There are several ways to upload a .docx, .doc, .rtf, or .txt file using the browser-based versions of Drive and Docs (this functionality is not available for the mobile apps):

Google Drive

1. In Google Drive's main screen, click the *New* button and *File upload*.

2. Navigate your hard drive to choose the .doc, .docx, .txt, or .rtf file that you want to import.

3. After uploading is complete, the file will appear in your *My Drive* list. Microsoft Word documents have a blue symbol next to them (a blue "W").

Google Docs (browser/Chromebook)

1. Click the *Open file picker* icon, which looks like a folder, and select *Upload*.

2. In the pop-up that appears, Click the *Select a file from your computer* button or drag the file you want to upload to the center of the pop-up.

3. Microsoft Word files should automatically be converted to Google Docs editor mode. If not, open the file and select *File > Open with Google Docs*.

Converting PDFs to Docs or Word

Some years ago, I created a short YouTube video that demonstrated how to convert a PDF to editable text using Google Docs. I thought it was a quirky little feature, but judging by the more than one hundred thousand people who have viewed the video, the feature is in high demand!

Follow the same steps as above to upload the PDF. Docs will attempt to parse the text. If successful, it will create a new Docs file with the extracted text, which can be edited, copied, or shared with other people.

A few notes about this method:

➤ It works best with PDF files that have been created by other word processors or layout programs, such as Microsoft Word or Adobe InDesign. It does not work with PDFs that were created with a scanner or camera.

➤ You can't edit the original PDF, only a Docs copy of the text.

➤ It will not preserve the original formatting of the PDF.

➤ Docs cannot parse large PDF files. Try splitting long PDFs into chunks of 20 pages or less before uploading to Google Docs.

Templates and more

There are additional features in Google Docs that beginners will find extremely useful. They include design, research, and collaboration tools.

Templates

Google Docs provides pre-existing templates for documents, spreadsheets and presentations. There are dozens available. I've used templates for invoices, résumés, and fax cover letters:

To use a template, do the following:

1. In an existing document, go to *File > New > From template.* Template options are also displayed from the Google Docs main screen.

2. Select one of the templates.

3. Change the title of the document. Formatting and other elements can be changed using the formatting toolbar.

4. Templates can also be activated from the Google Docs mobile apps for Android and iOS. Tap the plus icon, and select *Choose template.*

Translate Document

This feature will create a rough translation of your document in any language that Google Translate supports. It can give people who speak a different language a rough idea of what your document is about.

However, the quality of the translations is poor. It is not a substitute for a qualified human translator.

To use this feature:

1. Open your document.

2. Go to *Tools > Translate document.*

3. Select the language you want to translate your document to, and press the *Translate* button.

Explore, Collaboration, Offline Editing, and Add-ons

Google Docs has a neat feature called *Explore* which lets you quickly find information about a highlighted topic in your document. It also displays online images to insert into the document.

To use this feature, tap the Explore icon (which looks like a four-pointed star) or select *Tools > Explore.* A sidebar will appear with web and image results. Select an image and click *Insert* to add it to the document.

Collaboration lets users invite other people to collaboratively edit a document in real time. It has to be seen to be believed. Chapter 6 explains how to activate collaboration features.

Offline files is a very helpful feature for working in Docs while you are traveling or otherwise not connected to the Internet. Extra setup steps may be required, as described in Chapter 7.

Add-ons are small applications that work with Google Docs. To access them, select *Add-ons > Get add-ons.* Examples include a quick citation generator, a table of contents tool, table formatters, thesauruses, and even an online fax service.

CHAPTER 3

Google Sheets and Google Forms

Just as Google Docs duplicates much of the functionality of Microsoft Word, Google Sheets takes aim at Microsoft Excel.

While Google Sheets is good, it comes up short in a few key areas, such as formatting and working with large sets of data. That said, for basic calculations, charts, and sorting, Sheets is more than adequate. It's also easy to use, and comes with the following online sharing options that advanced users will appreciate:

➤ Integration with data from online sources.

➤ The ability to create online surveys using Google Forms.

➤ Online collaboration (see Chapter 6).

Since we only have a limited amount of time, I am going to show you how to get started with the basic features of Sheets. If you are relatively new to spreadsheet programs, it would be a good idea to open Sheets and try some of the simple exercises below. As with all of the exercises in this guide, I recommend using Sheets in the Google Chrome browser or on a Chromebook.

If you are interested in more advanced examples and instructions, *Excel Basics In 30 Minutes* covers Google Sheets and recent versions of Microsoft Excel. Visit *in30minutes.com* for more information.

How to create and rename spreadsheets

Making a new spreadsheet starts with the *New* button in Google Drive, or the plus icon in Google Sheets (see screenshot, below). Sheets automatically saves information as you type.

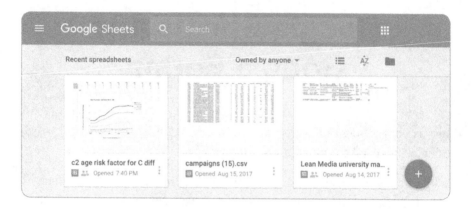

To rename a spreadsheet in the browser or Chromebook versions of Google Sheets, simply click on the name at the top of the browser window. If you are using the Google Sheets mobile app, tap the More Actions icon and select *Rename*.

Import options

Use Google Drive to import .xls and .xlsx files and convert them into Sheets files for editing, collaboration, and web forms.

If you are using Google Drive in a browser, follow these steps to import an Excel file:

1. Click the *New* button, and select *File upload*.

2. Locate the Excel file and select it.

3. Google Drive may automatically convert the Excel file to Google Sheets, depending on your settings. The newly converted spreadsheet will appear in *My Drive*. It will also be available in Google Sheets.

4. If the Excel file is not converted, open it in Google Sheets and select *File > Save as Google Sheets*.

If you are using the Google Drive mobile app, upload using the plus button and then open the file in the Google Sheets app. Press the More Actions icon, tap *Share & export*, and then select *Save as Google Sheets file*. Note that formatting and certain Excel functions may not be preserved during the conversion process.

Sheets allows limited editing of Microsoft Excel documents. It's possible to perform the following actions on Excel files in Google Sheets:

➤ Edit numbers and cell values.

➤ Apply limited formatting to selected cells.

➤ Manually type formulas and certain functions.

However, advanced Excel features and tools are not supported in Sheets.

Export options

Google Sheets can export files as .xlsx (Excel), OpenDocument (.ods), PDF, text, .csv (comma-separated values), .tsv (tab-separated values), and HTML. Open the spreadsheet in a browser or Chromebook, and select *File > Download as* to see the available options.

Export options for the Google Sheets app for Android and iOS are limited to .xlsx files. On the main screen of the app, follow these steps:

1. Tap the More Actions icon (three dots)

2. Select *Share & export*

3. Select *Save as Excel (.xlsx)*

Functions and calculations

Microsoft Excel, Google Sheets, and other spreadsheet programs were designed for crunching numbers. If you're used to Excel, the basic layout, commands and math/business functions carry over to Sheets.

However, the programs are not identical. Google has done a lot to streamline Sheets' interface, which makes it easy to perform simple calculations and tasks.

Another significant difference between Excel and Sheets: Excel has more power, and is better able to handle large spreadsheets. If you are working with an exceptionally large dataset (more than 500 rows or columns) the Sheets application may become unresponsive or may display errors. Past a certain point, you may even get a warning that Sheets is unable to add any more cells.

The next few exercises are intended for people who have never used Excel or any other spreadsheet program. Experienced users can skip ahead.

Spreadsheet terminology

When you create a new spreadsheet in Google Sheets, the grid on the screen is called a worksheet. A spreadsheet file can have more than one worksheet, and they will be layered on top of each other and accessible via tabs at the bottom of the grid.

The small rectangles that fill a worksheet are called cells. They are designed to hold numbers (for instance, 5, 26.2, $500 or 98%) as well as text ("Sarah", "Account past due", "245-BNX", column headers, etc.). Sometimes, people will use a cell to refer to other cells that are part of a formula (more on that later).

Because there are so many cells, worksheets use a simple system to identify each one. The top of each column is labeled with letters, while the rows running down the left side of the window are labeled with numbers. It's similar to the game Battleship, in which you identify a specific location on the grid by calling out *A7* or *J3*. If the worksheet has more than 26 columns, the 27th column is labeled AA, the 28th column is labeled AB, etc.

You can use arrow keys or sliders to move quickly around the worksheet. If you enter numbers or text into a cell, and the cell is not big enough to display the contents, the width of all cells in the same column can be adjusted by hovering the mouse over the dividing line between two cells until a tiny right-facing arrow appears. Grab the arrow with the mouse and drag it to the right or left to adjust the width of the column.

Your first formula

Let's do a quick exercise. You can use Google Sheets in a browser or a Chromebook, or use the mobile app for Android and iOS:

➤ Create a new spreadsheet in Google Sheets. Rename it "Sample spreadsheet" or any other name.

➤ Find cell A1. In it, type the number 65.2 and press *Return/Enter*. If you are using the Google Sheets app on your phone or tablet, select the cell and then use the Formula Bar (marked with *fx*) to enter the number.

➤ In cell A2, enter the number 42.

➤ In cell A3 enter the number 459.

Your worksheet should look like this:

	A	B	C	D	E
1	65.2				
2	42				
3	459				
4					
5					

Adding these numbers together in our heads would be slow, and we might make mistakes. Doing it with a pen and paper would be time-consuming. But spreadsheet formulas make it easy.

The formula will be placed in an empty cell that will calculate the total of the three cells. It can be the cell immediately below the numbers, or it can be a cell that's located several columns away. The calculation can be completed anywhere on the worksheet, and will refer back to the cells that contain the values to be added together.

Let's select a cell two columns over—cell C4. In it, type the following text. But don't press *Return/Enter* yet:

$$=A1+A2+A3$$

This is a formula. All formulas and functions entered into a spreadsheet have to start with an equal sign (=). It looks backwards, but starting with an equal sign tells Excel or Sheets that you are entering a formula or function, as opposed to typing text or numbers.

A1, A2, and A3 are references to the cells that contain numerical values. References can be typed as lowercase ("a3"), but Sheets will convert them to uppercase.

As you type each reference into your formula, the cell in question will have a colored rectangle drawn around it. The color of the text being typed changes color to match it.

The colored outlines verify that you are typing the correct cell references. For instance, if you mistakenly typed B3 instead of A3, an empty cell would be highlighted, instantly letting you know that you had entered the wrong cell reference.

As you type, you may also notice that the Formula Bar shows exactly what you are typing. Further, a preview of the result is shown in cell C4 as you expand the formula:

Press *Return/Enter*. The result of adding the three cells is shown in cell C4. Select cell C4 again. The number in the cell stays the same, but the Function Bar still displays the formula you entered. This is a handy way of determining how a cell's value was calculated.

How to create a series of numbers using Auto-fill

When you are working with spreadsheets, it's common to create a series of numbers in a row or column. For instance, you may need to make the top cell of each column show all years from 2015 through 2025. Typing each year would be time consuming and prone to error. Fortunately, there is an easy way to create a series of numbers in a spreadsheet. It's called *Auto-fill*. The following exercise for Google Sheets in a browser or a Chromebook demonstrates how Auto-fill works:

1. Create a new spreadsheet.

2. In the top row, type *1* in the cell A1.

3. Type *2* in cell B1.

4. Highlight both cells by dragging across the two cells with your mouse button held down.

5. On the lower right corner of cell B1, you will see a small blue square or dot. Grab it with your mouse, and drag to the right (see screenshot below).

6. Cell C1 will show the number 3, cell D1 will show the number 4, etc.

Google Sheets examples

| File | Edit | View | Insert | Format | Data | Tools | Add-ons | Help | All… |

🖶 ↶ ↷ 📋   100% ▾ $ % .0 .00 123 ▾   Arial ▾

fx | 1

	A	B	C	D	E
1	1	2	3	4	
2					
3					
4					
5					

Additional notes

1. The same function works for years, months (date or name), and days of the week (date or name).

2. You also can use Auto-fill to quickly generate results for mathematical functions and formulas across many columns (see example later in this chapter).

3. Clear the numbers in the spreadsheet by highlighting all cells and pressing the *Delete* key.

4. The Google Sheets app for Android and iOS devices does not support Auto-fill.

SUM and simple math functions

In the browser and Chromebook versions of Google Sheets, the *toolbar* is located above the worksheet. It contains buttons and drop-down menus for common commands and functions, which are alternate ways of expressing mathematical formulas. The Greek Sigma symbol is a drop-down menu for various math functions:

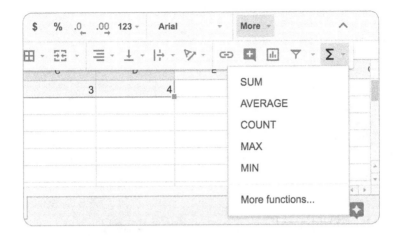

The toolbar and functions are not displayed in the Google Sheets app for Android and iOS, although it is possible to manually type the functions on mobile devices.

Here are some examples that use the SUM function:

Example: Single-column addition

1. In column A, type three single-digit numbers in the first three cells (A1, A2, and A3). You can use the same numbers from the previous exercise demonstrating formulas.

2. Highlight the cells.

3. Select the Sigma symbol to bring up a list of common math functions.

4. Select SUM.

5. In the cell A4 (see example below), you will see *=SUM(A1:A3)*. Sheets is asking, "Show the result for the sum of all numbers from cell A1 to cell A3?"

6. Press *Return/Enter* to confirm.

7. The sum of the three cells is shown in cell A4.

Example: Multiple column addition and average:

1. In column A, type three numbers in the first three rows (A1, A2, and A3).

2. In column B, type three different numbers in the first three rows (B1, B2, and B3).

3. In column C, type three more numbers in the first three rows (C1, C2, and C3).

4. Highlight cells in the first row (A1, A2, and A3). Do not highlight any other cells.

5. Select the Sigma symbol, and select SUM.

6. In the cell A4 (immediately below the highlighted cells), you will see =SUM(A1:A3).

7. Press *Return/Enter* on your keyboard to confirm.

8. The sum of the three cells is shown in cell A4.

9. Select cell A4 to highlight it.

10. You will see a small dot in the corner of cell A4. Grab it with your mouse and drag it to the right, over the empty cells B4 and C4.

11. Auto-fill will be activated. Cells B4 and C4 will show the totals of their respective columns.

	A	B	C	D	E
	🖨 ↰ ↱ ⊓ 100% ▾ $ % .0 .00 123 ▾ Arial ▾				
fx	=SUM(A1:A3)				
1	65.2	226	88.1		
2	42	3.55	104.1		
3	459	90	106.3		
4	566.2	319.55	298.5		
5					
6					

Example: To calculate the average of all three sums:

1. Highlight cells A4, B4, and C4.

2. Select the Sigma symbol, and select AVERAGE.

3. In cell D4, you will see *=AVERAGE(A4:C4)*.

4. Press *Return/Enter* on your keyboard to confirm.

5. The average will appear in cell D4.

	A	B	C	D	E
	🖨 ↰ ↱ ⊓ 100% ▾ $ % .0 .00 123 ▾ Arial ▾				
fx	=AVERAGE(A4:C4)				
1	65.2	226	88.1		
2	42	3.55	104.1		
3	459	90	106.3		
4	566.2	319.55	298.5	394.75	
5					

You can experiment with other functions. Common ones include:

➤ **COUNT:** Counts the number of highlighted cells with numerical data in them.

➤

> ➤ **MAX and MIN:** Displays the highest and lowest numerical value in the selected cells.

Additional notes

You can see a full list of functions by selecting *More functions* under the Sigma symbol. The list is exhaustive and covers mathematical, business, and practical functions. For instance, Example: *=TODAY( )* displays today's date in the cell.

As with Excel, it's possible to combine/nest functions in Sheets. Here's an example:

=SUM(A1:A3)+AVERAGE(B1:B3)

This function will add the sum of the first column of numbers to the average of the second column of numbers.

For complicated functions or nested functions, I often type them in a different text editor and then paste them into Sheets. It's quicker to make changes this way.

All functions must begin with an equal sign (=). Using the wrong type of data in a function will also generate errors. Example: Attempting to use *AVERAGE( )* on a column and mistakenly including the header text in the range will generate an error, because text cannot be averaged.

Formatting numbers and cells

The toolbar in Sheets will contain many familiar buttons to change formatting. Some are the same as those used in Docs—for example, buttons to bold or align the contents of a cell, or increase the font size.

Numbers have their own formatting buttons. They include:

> ➤ **Dollar:** Instantly formats a number in U.S. dollars. To select another nation's currency, go to *Format > Number > More formats > More currencies.*

> ➤ **%:** Instantly converts the data to a percentage.

➤ **123:** Selects other formats, including:

▷ Round up to the nearest whole number.

▷ Round to two decimal places.

▷ Round to *n* decimal places.

➤ **Financial**

▷ *Example:* –1000 rendered as (1,000)

➤ **Scientific**

▷ *Example:* –1000 rendered as –1.00E+03

➤ **Dates and Times**

Sorting and filtering data

These powerful features, enabled through the *Filter* button, let users pick out pieces of data from large datasets and order them. An example would be reordering the rows from highest to lowest based on the values in column C.

Without getting too technical, here are some basic examples:

Temperatures example

Let's take a look at the high temperatures for four U.S. cities over a single week. The first view shows the raw data:

	A	B	C	D	E	F
1		Boston	New York	Philadelphia	Buffalo	
2	Sunday	29	32	34	20	
3	Monday	32	34	34	18	
4	Tuesday	25	23	28	18	
5	Wednesday	24	24	30	20	
6	Thursday	26	28	29	22	
7	Friday	35	36	33	28	
8	Saturday	33	33	31	29	
9						

To sort the New York temperatures from warmest to coldest, select column C by tapping or clicking the letter "C." Then, select *Data > Sort sheet by column C, Z to A.* This tells Sheets to rearrange the values in column C from largest to smallest. The rest of the values in other columns will automatically adjust so the Friday temperatures are on top (Friday was the warmest day in New York) and Tuesday is on the bottom.

It's also possible to show the data filtered for those days when the temperature in Buffalo was 20 degrees:

	A	B	C	D	E	F
		Boston	New York	Philadelphia	Buffalo	
1						
2	Sunday	29	32	34	20	
5	Wednesday	24	24	30	20	
9						
10						
11						
12						
13						

fx Buffalo

100% $ % .0 .00 123 Arial 10

To duplicate the above results from the original raw data, the following steps are required:

1. In column E, under the *Buffalo* heading, select the first cell that contains the number 20 (cell E2).

2. Select *Data > Filter.*

3. Triangular icons will appear at the top of every column. Click the triangle at the top of column E to display the *Sort/Filter* options.

4. Clear the checkmarks next to the numbers (which correspond to the data in that column).

5. Select *20,* and press the *OK* button.

It's easy to imagine how these features could be used to quickly isolate and order data from large lists. Examples include:

➤ **Listing the highest-paid workers** in a department with hundreds of employees.

➤ **Identifying struggling students** in a large high school, based on grades.

➤ **Tracking a transaction** in a list of thousands of sales records, based on a specific amount.

How to make a manual list

If you've manually built lists in Excel, you can do the same thing in Sheets.

1. In the top row, enter your headers that describe the data. In a training session scenario, the headers might be *Last Name, First Name, Department*, etc.

2. Manually enter the data. A typical scenario would involve the owner of the spreadsheet gradually entering the data as people sign up via email or phone.

3. Manipulate the data. Filter and Sort can really help, especially for large lists (Boss: "Get me a list of staff whose last name begins with the letter 'N', pronto!").

Charts and graphs

Sheets can generate simple charts and graphs. For people who are familiar with Excel's powerful graphing features, Google's tools may seem primitive. But they are more than adequate for basic uses.

How to make a chart or graph

At a very basic level, making a graph involves selecting a group of data and pressing the *Insert chart* button on the Sheets toolbar (select the *More* button if you don't see it).

In the following example, I've selected all of the cells in the Weekly High Temperatures spreadsheet, and then pressed the *Insert chart* button, which brings up the *Chart editor* window. Sheets recommends the following chart:

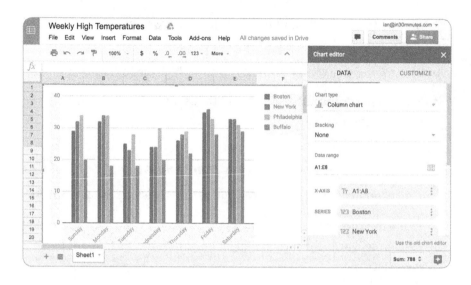

However, the thin, colorful lines aren't suitable, as they make it difficult to compare temperatures in specific cities from day to day. By exploring the other chart options, I found a simple line chart without any fill colors:

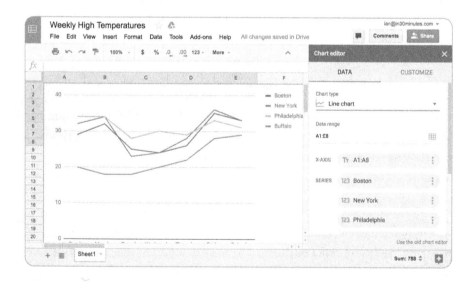

To edit a chart, select it to make the *Chart editor* appear, and then select the *Customize* tab. Scroll through *Title*, *Series*, and *Legend* to change fonts, colors, orientation, and other elements. Title text can be changed by selecting the title on the chart and typing. Use the More Actions icon (three dots) to copy or delete the chart, or save an image file.

Note that certain types of charts require certain types of spreadsheet data in order to work. For instance, columns that contain lists of names cannot be used to make line, bar, or pie charts, because these types of charts require numbers, not text.

Taking spreadsheets to the next level with Google Forms

While early spreadsheet programs were created to help businesses with their finances, office workers soon found another use: entering text into cells to make lists.

For instance, someone might create a list of the names and departments of attendees at a training session, or the participants in an office betting pool, and then manipulate the data using filtering and sorting functions.

Google Forms takes the list concept a step further with a form creation tool that puts custom forms on the web and feeds the data into Google Sheets.

How to use Google Forms to gather data

Google Forms is a tool to build online forms, which can then be emailed, shared on social media, or embedded on a public-facing website. The forms can really change the way you gather data. Think about it: Instead of manually entering data, you can make a simple form or survey, post it on the web, and let other people do the work for you!

This tool is perfect for signup forms and simple reporting. However, I have found some buggy behavior in a limited number of data-entry scenarios. Always test a form before sharing it with other people to make sure it works as expected.

Once a form has been created, it can be accessed via a Google link that you can email or post on a social network. The form can also be embedded on a blog or company web page. Customization options can make the form look more professional, or let you match the fonts and colors you want to use. The data from the form is only visible to you and designated collaborators.

The instructions below apply to the updated interface for creating new forms.

How to create a form

1. You can either use an existing spreadsheet (select *Tools > Create a form*) or make a new form from Google Drive's main screen by pressing the *New* button and selecting *More > Google Forms*.

2. The form editor appears (see screenshot, below).

3. Enter the title.

4. Enter the description. Make it clear what the form is being used for, and add any instructions that can help people complete the form. Absent context or appropriate instructions, users may be reluctant to use the form, or they may enter the wrong type of data.

5. Edit the first untitled question. Change the name of the question by selecting the title. Change option labels by clicking on them. Select different question types from the drop-down menu. Select *Required* to force users to answer a question.

6. Add a new question using the *Add question* button. There are more than a half-dozen types of questions that can be used.

   ➤ *Short answer*. A one-line text field.

   ➤ *Paragraph*. Allows for longer answers.

   ➤ *Multiple choice*. Create a multiple-choice question, with as many possible answers as you want.

   ➤ *Checkboxes*. People can check off one or more items from a list.

   ➤ *Dropdown*. Creates a drop-down menu.

   ➤ *Linear scale*. Users choose from a range of numbers.

   ➤ *Multiple choice grid*. Users fill in data according to a table.

   ➤ *Date or Time*. Users can select the date or time (useful for scheduling purposes).

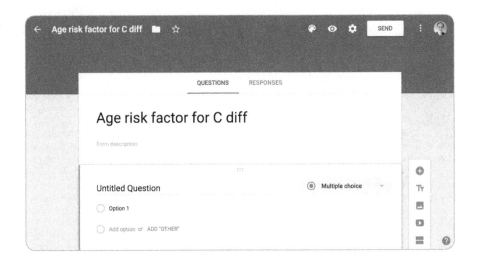

The form builder has additional functions:

➤ Icons allow form creators to add titles, sections, photos, and video.

➤ Change the colors used in the form by selecting the easel icon.

➤ Preview the form by selecting the eye icon.

➤ The settings icon (which looks like a gear) controls who can use the form, as well as presentation options. Use the drop-down menu to select *Anyone* or one of the other options, if available.

When complete, press the *Send* button, which shows various distribution options. Email is the default choice, but social media icons, web links, and embed code (which can be used to insert the form into a blog post) are other possibilities.

Data entered into the web form can be accessed via the *Responses* tab at the top of the form editor. Click the Sheets icon to flow the data into a new or existing spreadsheet, which can then be formatted, sorted, filtered and otherwise manipulated. To return to a form, search for it in Google Drive or visit *https://docs.google.com/forms*.

CHAPTER 4

Google Slides

A few chapters ago, I described Google Docs as an adequate substitute for Microsoft Word. And while Google Sheets isn't nearly as slick as Excel, it covers the basics as well as advanced features such as online forms.

Now we come to Slides, the Google equivalent of Microsoft PowerPoint. Slides is the runt of the litter. Yes, it handles all of the things you would expect in a standard slideshow application, from animations to themes. But the presentations don't look sophisticated—a potential negative for business users.

In business presentations, positive impressions can help make a sale or win over an audience. PowerPoint and Apple's Keynote software, when used properly, can be extremely effective tools for business communication. But Slides, with its flat designs and simple templates, looks too basic. It may be enough for a student project or a presentation to a local community group, but for serious business, Slides' primitive designs can actually be a distraction for people who are used to slick PowerPoint decks.

Nevertheless, Slides does have a few saving graces:

➤ Its relative lack of features makes it very easy to use.

➤ Collaboration is easier.

➤ Slides can be instantly ported to the web.

➤ It's possible to create, edit, and present Slides offline.

➤ It's possible to create a draft Slides file to take advantage of Google's collaboration features, and then export the file to PowerPoint for more sophisticated animations and formatting.

Google has also done a lot to improve Google Slides on mobile devices. When I wrote the first edition of this guide, Slides was basically limited to laptop and desktop computers. Now, the Google Slides app for phones and tablets is a superb tool for making quick edits while on the go, or even giving impromptu presentations without having to break out the laptop and projector. You can actually use the Google Slides app to give a 30-second elevator pitch in an elevator, using nothing more than your Android or iOS phone!

Over the next few pages, I'll introduce the basic features of Slides.

Creating and launching presentations

To create a new presentation in Google Slides, use one of the following methods:

➤ **Google Drive:** *New > Google Slides*

➤ **Google Slides** (browser, Chromebook, or app): Press the plus symbol to create a new file.

If you are creating a new presentation using the browser or Chromebook versions of Google Slides, you will be prompted to choose a template:

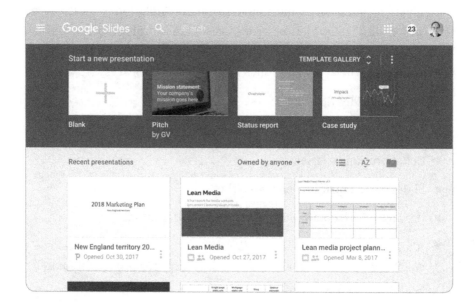

The Google Slides app for phones and tablets now has the ability to change themes and insert images, shapes, and tables. However, advanced features such as editing animations are not supported.

The browser and Chromebook versions of Google Slides save automatically as you add text, formatting, and other elements. The Google Slides mobile app may require tapping the checkmark icon to save certain changes.

A presentation can be launched using the following methods:

➤ **Browser/Chromebook:** Press the *Present* button in the upper-right corner of the toolbar area.

➤ **Mobile app:** Tap the triangular Play icon at the top of the screen (see screenshot, below).

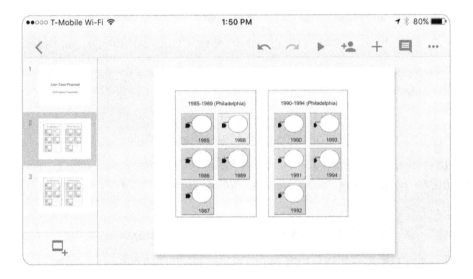

While Microsoft PowerPoint files can be launched within Google Slides, note that the original formatting and animations may not be reflected in the presentation that plays on the screen. For this reason, I advise launching .ppt and .pptx files using PowerPoint, which is part of Microsoft Office. There is also a very powerful and free mobile PowerPoint app for Android and iOS devices (to learn more, check out *PowerPoint Basics In 30 Minutes* by author Angela Rose).

How to import and convert PowerPoint files

While Google Slides can import and export PowerPoint files (.ppt and .pptx), formatting does not translate well. This is a significant issue for users who attempt to convert a beautiful PowerPoint presentation. Colors, fonts, shadows, and other elements may appear drastically different in Slides. Animations may not work at all.

Fortunately, Google Slides has enabled limited editing of PowerPoint slides (see *Direct editing of Microsoft Office formats* in Chapter 1). This makes it possible to make simple text and formatting changes in an imported PowerPoint file without having to convert it to Google Slides.

To import a .ppt or .pptx file using the browser and Chromebook versions of Google Slides, follow these steps:

1. Open Google Drive, select *New* and select *Upload files*.

2. Find the PowerPoint files (.ppt or .pptx) that you want to use in Slides.

3. A box will appear on the screen, notifying you that the upload is taking place.

4. Once completed, the PowerPoint files can be identified by the "P" icon in the list of files on Google Drive or in Google Slides.

To convert an imported PowerPoint file to Slides format for editing, open the file by selecting *File > Open with Google Slides*.

How to export a presentation

To export or convert a Google Slides presentation, use *File > Download as* in the browser or Chromebook versions of Google Slides. Presentations can be converted to the following formats:

➤ **PowerPoint** *(.pptx)*. Note that formatting may not be preserved in the exported .pptx file.

➤ **PDF.** The PDF will look similar to the original presentation, but animations and transitions are not supported. Text and images cannot be edited.

➤ **Image formats.** Individual slides can be exported as .jpg, .png, or .svg files.

➤ **Text.** Exported files will contain the text of the original spreadsheet, but no other elements.

If you are using an Android or Apple phone or tablet, export options are limited to PowerPoint files. To access this feature, tap the More Actions icon (three dots) and select *Share & export > Save as PowerPoint (.pptx)*.

How to add slides to a presentation

To create a new slide, follow these steps:

Browser/Chromebook

1. Press the button with a plus symbol in the upper left corner of the toolbar, or use the keyboard shortcut *Ctrl-M.*

2. The drop-down menu next to the plus button lets you choose various formats ("blank", "title with two columns", etc.)

If you have created a complicated slide or formatting that you want to reproduce on another slide, use *Insert > Duplicate* and delete the text and elements you no longer need.

Android/iOS

1. Tap the *Add slide* button.

2. Choose a blank slide or one of the preformatted slide options.

Editing features of Google Slides

When editing a presentation in the browser or Chromebook versions of Google Slides, a toolbar runs across the top, and thumbnails of the slides appear on the left side of the screen. The selected slide will occupy the center of the screen:

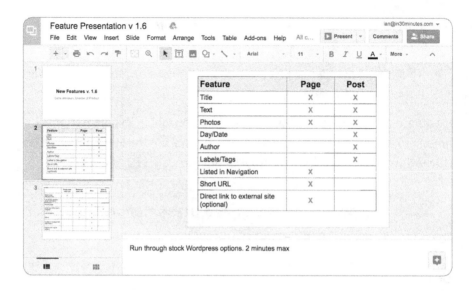

To display toolbars in the mobile app, tap a text box or shape to see basic options. Press the icon with the letter A to format text or shapes. Use the plus icon to insert images, shapes, lines, and tables.

As noted earlier, the appearance of the presentations in Google Slides doesn't hold a candle to a well-designed PowerPoint deck. On the other hand, the learning curve for Slides is gentle—Google has made it very easy to create, edit, and format presentations.

How to change a theme

When you create a new presentation, you can work with a blank presentation or select a pre-made template. You can also change *themes*, which are combinations of colors, fonts, background images, and other style elements. For instance, the *Modern* theme is simply a white background with a black bar for the subtitle.

To change the theme in the browser or Chromebook versions of Google Slides, select the *Theme* button on the default toolbar. When using the Slides app on your phone or tablet, select the More Actions icon (three dots) and then *Change theme*.

How to format elements in Slides

I recommend using the browser or Chromebook versions of Google Slides to perform formatting changes. The mobile app simply doesn't have much flexibility when it comes to formatting text and other presentation elements, and on small-screen devices, manipulating individual elements can be difficult.

The Slides toolbar has two configurations. When you open an existing presentation, or create a new one, it will look like this:

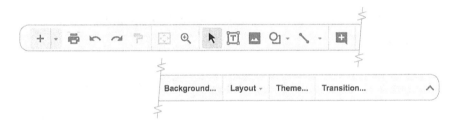

The buttons can create new text boxes, lines, and shapes, and can also bring up the settings for backgrounds, themes, transitions and animations.

However, once text or some other item on the slide is selected with the mouse or trackpad, the formatting toolbar appears:

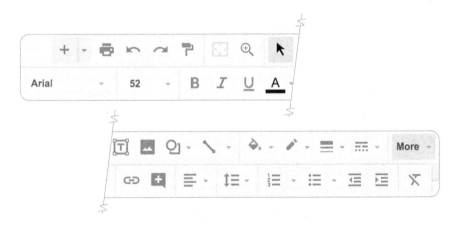

The text formatting options (bold, italics, font size, etc.) should be familiar. (For a refresher, please refer to Chapter 2). Unlike PowerPoint, Google Slides does not have options for adding text shadows or other sophisticated effects.

Additional buttons include:

➤ **Fill color** (paint bucket icon). Pressing this button shows a color palette. Selecting a color will change the background color of the selected box or graphic element.

➤ **Border or line color** (crayon button). This changes the color of drawn lines and arrows, text boxes, and edges of shapes such as squares and ovals.

➤ **Line weight.** Changes the thickness of a line, arrow, or shape edge.

➤ **Line dash.** Turns a line, arrow or edge of an element from a solid line to a dashed line.

How to add new lines, boxes, and other elements

The Google Slides toolbar has buttons for creating the following elements:

➤ **Text boxes**

➤ **Images**

➤ **Lines and arrows** (includes curves, polylines, and scribbles).

➤ **Shapes** (boxes, cylinders, callout bubbles, large symbols, etc.).

The method for creating each of these elements is basically the same:

1. Press the button for the box/element you want to draw.

2. Crosshairs will appear on the slide area.

3. Hold down the mouse button and drag to draw the element.

4. When the element is the desired size, let go.

5. You may need to click outside the line or shape to complete it.

How to manipulate slide elements

To manually change the position of text, images, graphics boxes, or any other graphic element, follow these steps:

1. Make sure the *Select* tool (the toolbar button that looks like an arrow) is active.

2. Select the box or element you want to move.

3. Move the square dots that appear along the corners and edges to expand/reduce/change the shape.

4. To move the element, hover the mouse over the edge of the element, then "grab" it to move it.

5. Elements that are partially moved off the slide's surface will be cut off when the presentation is launched.

To move multiple shapes at once, make sure Select is active, and draw a rectangle that touches all of the items you want to move. The items will all be highlighted at the same time. Use your mouse to move the connected objects around the screen.

Text boxes and other shapes can be rotated by grabbing the dot above a selected shape and moving the mouse. When it looks good, release the dot.

Transitions and animations

Slides has animation options that can control the appearance and exit of elements on the page, as well as the transitions between slides. These cannot be edited using the mobile app, so the following instructions apply to the browser and Chromebook versions of Google Slides.

How to create transitions

To get started, open a presentation in Slides and navigate to the slide you want to animate. Press the *Transitions* button in the toolbar (if you don't see the *Transitions* button, select the slide thumbnail on the left side of the screen, or select the *More* button and then *Transitions*). The Animations pane will appear on the right side of the screen:

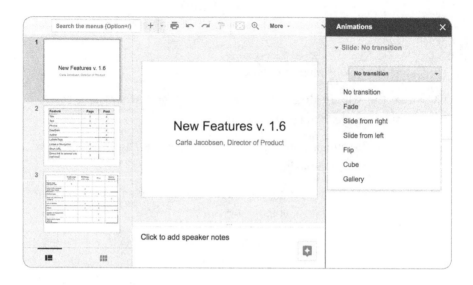

At the top of the pane below the *Slide* selector are transitions, which determine how the next slide will appear when the presentation is launched. A standard presentation might fade between slides, but if you're feeling adventurous, you can select *Flip* or *Cube*. Press the *Apply to all slides* button to have the chosen effect work with all of your slides.

How to create animations

Below the transitions options are animations for individual elements within a slide. Select an item on the page to get started, and then select *Add animation* (if the Animations pane is not visible, select *Insert > Animation*). Options include fading, flying, and appearing/disappearing.

The *On click* drop-down menu controls how the animation will be activated.

➤ **On click** means an animation will start when the presenter clicks the mouse.

➤ **With previous** means the animation will follow the animation for another element on the screen. This is useful if you want several items to simultaneously appear or leave the screen.

The speed of each animation can also be adjusted, using the slider.

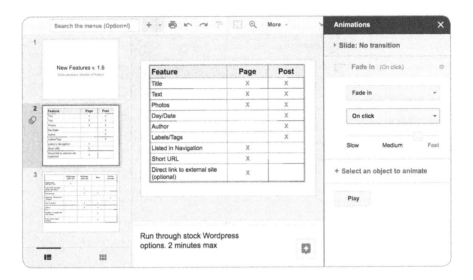

Online options

Besides collaboration (explained in Chapter 6), one of the most powerful options for Slides is the ability to publish on the web. Google handles the hosting. You can easily email or share the link with others, or even embed the presentation on a company website or blog.

This is a very easy way to do a live presentation over the phone, or have a non-collaborator remotely review a presentation. You can also use this option as a demonstration tool, creating a slideshow that will automatically rotate through the slides and then start over from the beginning.

How to publish a presentation on the web

To place a Slides presentation online so other people can see it, open the presentation and then select *File > Publish to the web*. A pop-up window will appear (see screenshot, below).

Under *Link* is a *Publish* button. Pressing it makes the presentation available online, using the highlighted link. There are options for auto-advancing the presentation when it is opened in a browser. Select *Embed* if you want to copy the code to place the presentation on a webpage or blog.

Under *Published content & settings* is another button to start or stop the online availability of the presentation. If you are using a G Suite domain, you may also see options to restrict the presentation to users of your domain. However, if you are using a standard Google Account, the link can be viewed by any person who has the link. This means that the link can be shared and forwarded, but it won't show up in search results.

CHAPTER 5

Google Drawings, Google Sites, and third-party apps

Google Drive comes with several additional programs, as well as the option to download compatible apps from other developers. The program that deserves a special mention is Google Drawings, a diagramming and sketching tool included with Google Drive.

What can you do with Drawings?

Drawings is integrated into Google Docs and Google Sheets (via the *Insert > Drawing* menu command), but there is also an option of using Drawings as a standalone program. It's very useful. I've used Drawings to create:

➤ **Diagrams** for online articles.

➤ **Flow models** for business presentations (see example, below).

➤ **Wireframes** for planning web and software applications.

➤ **Annotations** for imported images.

➤ **Simple maps.**

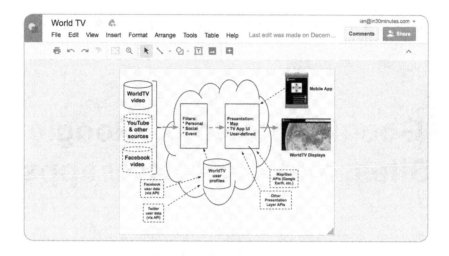

Creating a new drawing is easy. Press the *New* button in Drive and select *More > Google Drawings*. Specific capabilities are described below.

How to create objects in Drawings

After you've created a new drawing, you will be presented with a blank canvas and a toolbar. The buttons may look familiar—Google Slides uses a similar set for inserting objects like text boxes, shapes, lines and arrows. Indeed, the ways in which you create these objects in Drawings are the same:

1. Press the button for the box/element you want to draw. Additional options for each element are available via the drop-down menu attached to the buttons.

2. Crosshairs will appear in the drawing area.

3. Hold down the mouse button and drag to draw the element.

4. When the element is the desired size, let go. Elements can be moved, rotated, and resized using the dots around the edges of a selected shape (see *How to manipulate slide elements* in the previous chapter).

Google Drawings has an additional object type, Word Art, which is useful for making simple signs. Although both text boxes and Word Art can be used to "draw" text, Word Art text is treated as a graphic object. This means you can change line width, fill color and the shape of the Word Art as you would a circle or other shape (see test drawing, below).

How to delete objects in Drawings

If you make a mistake:

➤ Use the *Undo* button (the toolbar icon that looks like a curved arrow pointing left)

➤ Alternatively, select *Edit > Undo*.

To delete a single object:

1. Press the *Select* button.

2. Click once on the item you want to delete.

3. Press the *Delete* button on your keyboard, or use *Edit > Delete*.

If you want to get rid of several objects at once:

1. Press the *Select* button.

2. Draw a rectangle that overlaps the objects you want to delete and let go of the mouse.

3. The objects will all be selected and joined by a large rectangle.

4. Press the *Delete* button on your keyboard, or use *Edit > Delete*.

The new Google Sites

For years, users have been pleading for Google to turn Google Sites, a rudimentary online publishing platform, into something more. Googlers listened, and recently released a new version of Sites that contains some very powerful tools for sharing content created in Docs, Sheets, Slides, and YouTube. It's perfect for teachers and small organizations looking for a simple online publishing tool.

Note, however, that Sites requires users to post content to URLs beginning with sites.google.com. As of this writing, it is not possible to create a web-site in Sites that publishes to a custom domain.

Creating a new site

Press the *New* button in Google Drive, and then *More > Google Sites*. You'll be brought to a screen that shows a blank title and site name. Select these elements to enter text, and then use the Insert tool on the right side of the screen to place content below the title. (For instance, a teacher could create an assignment page that includes videos from YouTube and spreadsheet data from Google Sheets.)

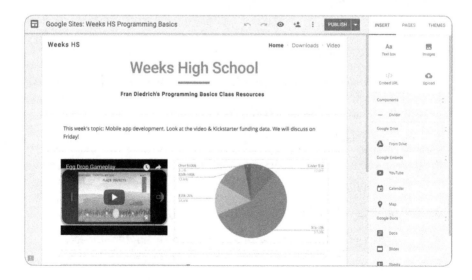

Content types include:

➤ Text boxes

➤ Uploaded images

➤ Public YouTube videos

➤ Google Calendars

➤ Google Maps

➤ Google Docs, Sheets, Slides, and Forms

➤ Charts created in Sheets

➤ Other content from Google Drive

To create a new page, switch to the *Pages* tool (look for the tab next to *Insert*). Each new page will automatically create a navigation link on the site once it's published.

There are limited options to customize the appearance of the content:

➤ As you hover over a piece of content, look for the palette icon. This changes that section's background by applying different emphasis and color schemes. You can also upload a background image.

➤ Boxes can be resized by grabbing the corners, or moved to another location by dragging them with the mouse.

➤ There are different text types (normal, title, heading, and subheading) and it's possible to apply bold, italics, or centered text.

➤ Insert dividers to separate content blocks.

It's not possible to change fonts or base colors unless you change the theme, using the Theme tab next to the Insert and Pages tools. Even then, choices will be limited.

To publish on Sites, press the *Publish* button. For free Google accounts, the site URL will be publicly viewable, although there is an option to hide it from most search engines. Paid G Suite accounts can also restrict the site to people using a paid email service purchased through Google.

Accessing other apps in Google Drive

Independent developers and other companies have built free apps that greatly extend the capabilities of Google Drive, Docs, Sheets, and Slides. Examples include:

➤ **HelloFax** lets you fax documents and PDFs stored in Google Drive.

➤ **Conceptboard** is a whiteboarding tool and visual collaboration platform for marketing and remote teams.

➤ **Drive Notepad** is a simple text editor for jotting down notes, pasting information, writing computer code, or for use as a scratchpad. Notes are saved in Google Drive and can be printed using Google Cloud Print.

There are dozens of other applications that let users convert between formats, make Gantt charts, edit audio and video, and even check the weather.

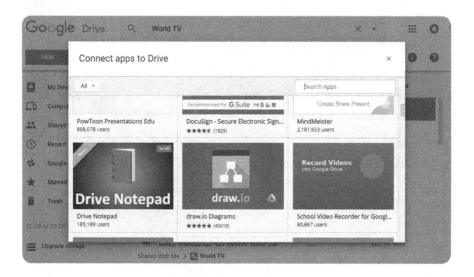

How to download other apps

To add third-party apps to your Drive account, take the following steps:

1. Open Google Drive.

2. Press *New* and then *More > Connect more apps*. A pop-up window will display some of the available apps that can be connected to your Google Drive account (see screenshot, above).

3. Choose the app you want to install.

4. Follow the onscreen instructions to complete installation.

Once the app is associated with your Google Drive account, you will be able to create new files from the app. Note that some apps may require additional registration steps or a subscription to use premium features.

Press *the New* button, and then *More* to make a new file or open the app.

CHAPTER 6

Collaboration

As a graduate student, I often worked on group projects. "Collaboration" usually involved emailing Word and Excel attachments, or passing USB drives containing files to classmates. It was clumsy and difficult to manage. It was also prone to error and wasted effort if people independently opened and worked on copies of the same file.

Then someone showed me how to collaborate using the *Share* feature in Docs. I don't recall what the report was about. But I vividly remember going to Google Docs, opening a document at the same time other students were working on it, and seeing their differently colored cursors moving around the screen, typing new words and making edits in real time. It was an epiphany.

Sharing is not limited to Docs. This chapter will explain how to enable online collaboration in other Google applications.

What to expect when collaborating in Google Drive

One of the great benefits of collaboration in Google's online office suite is that everyone works with the same copy of the file. It's possible for two or more people to simultaneously work on the same data, and for each to see what others are adding, changing, or deleting right on the screen.

This greatly reduces the chances of a document being forked—that is, being split into separate versions, with different editing histories. Forked documents can cause huge problems when it's time to reconcile the different versions of the file.

Different modes of collaboration

When working with other people on shared files in a browser, the collaboration may be live, with users working at the same time on a shared document. *Live collaboration* will seem strange at first. The cursors move around the screen without you controlling them. They may select, add, or delete text. Once you get the hang of it, live collaboration will become easy and efficient. Older ways of collaborating, such as emailing attachments back and forth, will seem primitive by comparison.

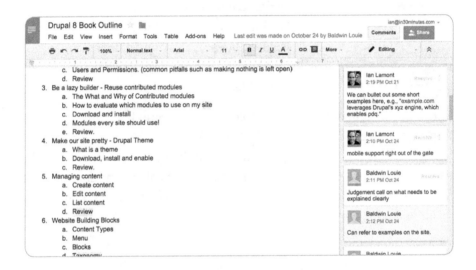

People don't have to collaborate simultaneously, though. If collaborators are working on the file at different times during the day (typical for teams with people in different time zones or countries), the changes will be saved as each user works on the document for the next user to see. Collaborators can also leave comments (see screenshot, above).

Setting up collaboration

Google has made it very easy to invite collaborators to work on a file or folder using email. Those who already have Google Accounts can begin to work on the shared file or folder right away. People who don't have Google Accounts will quickly be taken through the registration process.

It's also possible to grant access to people who don't have Google Accounts or don't use email to share a document on the web for anyone to see or edit.

While any file stored in Google Drive can be shared with other people, they won't be able to make edits unless it's in a Google format, such as Docs or Sites.

Microsoft Office documents, when opened in Docs, Sheets, and Slides, also show a *Share* button. But true collaboration is not possible—pressing the button merely shows a prompt to convert the documents to the corresponding Google format for editing and collaboration.

How to invite collaborators

To get started with collaboration using the Google Chrome browser or a Chromebook, follow these steps:

1. Open the Google file.

2. Select the *Share* button or go to *File > Share*.

3. The *Sharing settings* pop-up window will appear (see below).

4. Enter the email addresses of collaborators in the *Invite people* field.

5. Use the drop-down menu to the right of the field to control their access. This will determine if they can edit a document, add comments, or only view the contents.

6. To add a personal message to the notification email they receive, start typing in the *Add a message* field.

7. Press the *Done* button.

Here's what the *Sharing settings* pop-up looks like:

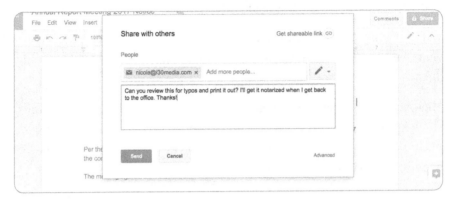

The *owner* of a file or folder is the person who created it. Only he or she can permanently *delete* a file or folder, or transfer ownership to another account via the *Share* button or icon. *Editors* are allowed to invite collaborators to a file or folder, or can enable public access.

Sharing on a phone or tablet

If you are using the Android or iOS app and want to enable sharing, simply follow these steps:

1. Open the file in question and tap the *Add people* icon, which looks like the silhouette of a person.

2. Type the name or email address of the collaborator. Potential matches from your device's address book may be shown below the field—simply tap to select.

3. Select the permission level (*Can edit, Can comment, Can view*).

4. Add an optional note.

5. Tap the *Add* button to send the invitation.

How to enable public editing

In most collaboration scenarios, only a select group of people are supposed to contribute to a document. Enabling public editing is less common, but it can be helpful for community projects, public education, or situations in which anonymous input is desired.

Here's how to enable public editing. Note that this can only be enabled from a browser or Chromebook:

1. While logged in, open the file in question, and press the *Share* button, or choose *File > Share*.

2. Select *Advanced*.

3. Next to *Specific people can access*, select *Change*.

4. Choose *Public on the web* to let anyone on the web find and access the shared file, or *Anyone with the link* to let people you manually notify access the file. No sign-in is required for either option.

5. G Suite users may see other options to restrict sharing to people in the same domain.

6. The default permission is *Can view*. Use the drop-down to allow editing or commenting by others.

7. Press *Save*. The link to share the document will be highlighted.

8. Press *Done* to return to editing the document.

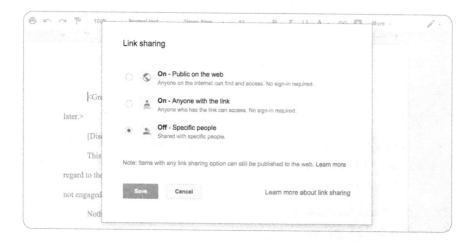

How to share a Google Drive folder

If you have a lot of documents that you need to share with colleagues, class-mates, or others, you'll want to use Google Drive's sharing features. Put all the relevant files into a single folder in Drive, and then share that folder. It's much easier than sharing one file at a time.

Sharing folders is something that can be done using the browser or Chrome-book versions of Google Drive. First, create a folder, and place files in it:

1. Go to *drive.google.com*, and press *New > Folder*. Name the folder. You can also use New > *Folder upload* to upload an existing folder on your hard drive. Note that this may take some time if there is a lot of data in the folder.

2. Add additional files by using *New > File upload* or dragging and drop-ping them into the folder to be shared.

Once the folder is ready, select it in Google Drive's home screen and select the Share icon (which looks like a silhouette), or right-click and select *Share*. Follow the same directions used for sharing a file with collaborators, described in *How to invite collaborators* earlier in this chapter.

How to remove collaborators from a file or folder

There's a personnel crisis at work. Francis in accounting is suspected of being a corporate spy! You need to lock down access to a shared spreadsheet, pronto!

It's easy to do using a browser or Chromebook:

1. Open the spreadsheet in Google Sheets, and select the *Share* button.

2. In the *Share with others* pop-up, select *Advanced*.

3. In the *Sharing settings* pop-up, click the "X" next to Francis' name.

4. To prevent public access, make sure *Link sharing* is turned off. If it is not, select the *Change* link next to the permissions row, and choose *Shared with specific people*.

Sharing settings for existing users currently cannot be accessed from the Android and iOS apps.

Contacting collaborators

Consider these common scenarios associated with collaborating on a shared file or folder:

➤ You want to make sure everyone has reviewed a document, spreadsheet, or presentation before printing it.

➤ Someone says he or she can't find a shared document.

➤ You're the owner of a shared file that you want to delete or unshare.

The easy way to handle these scenarios is to notify collaborators via email from within the document. This works best using the browser or Chromebook versions of the applications:

1. Open the file.

2. Go to *File > Email collaborators.*

3. The *Send message* pop-up will appear.

4. Select the people you want to notify using the checkboxes on the right.

5. Add a message.

6. Hit the *Send* button.

This function is not currently supported in the mobile apps for Android and iOS.

CHAPTER 7

Offline access and file storage

Google Drive is an application that lives in "the cloud." This is another way of saying "Internet-connected servers and systems for storing and processing large amounts of data." You access Drive and your files with a web browser or mobile app, though Google's cloud servers handle most of the heavy lifting when it comes to storage, conversion, and processing.

But there are ways of accessing extended functionality to a PC or Mac that is not connected to the Internet. It's even possible to edit certain types of files, including documents in Google Docs, and presentations in Google Slides.

The next few pages will explain how offline access works, and will also describe how to manage files and storage using the Google Drive application for PCs and Macs.

Working offline

If you are using a desktop computer, laptop, phone, or tablet connected to the Internet or a fast mobile network, your files can be accessed by visiting *drive.google.com* in a web browser or the Google Drive app.

What if you're not connected to the Internet?

When I was writing the first draft of this book in Google Docs, I sometimes had to work offline when I took the subway. At other times, my Wi-Fi connection would cut out in the middle of writing. It didn't matter—Doc's offline editing feature let me continue working. When I reconnected wirelessly, the changes were automatically updated on Google Drive.

How to set up offline editing

If you are using a Chromebook, offline editing works with Docs, Sheets, Slides, and Drawings right out of the box. For PCs or Macs, the Google Chrome browser is required for offline access, and you will need to install a separate Google Drive application on your computer. You may also need to activate offline access in the settings area:

1. While Chrome is connected to the Internet, open Drive and select the settings icon (the gear icon in the upper right corner) and then *Settings*.

2. Make sure the *Offline access* checkbox is checked.

To access the files, simply open Chrome and type *drive.google.com* into the address bar.

> **Protip:** PDFs, Microsoft Office files, and other files in your Google Drive account will not be available for offline editing. However, they can still be opened via the Google Drive folder on your hard drive if you have synced them via the Google Drive application for PCs and Macs (see below).

Mobile access

The Android and iOS apps for Drive, Docs, Sheets, and Slides allow offline access, but access has to be set for individual files while the device is connected to the Internet:

➤ **Android:** Tap the More Actions icon (three dots) next to the file and select *Available offline.*

➤ **iOS:** Tap the More Actions icon and select *Available offline* or *Keep.*

Working with offline files and storage in Google Drive

Besides Docs, Sheets, and the other programs described earlier in this book, Google Drive comes with enough free storage space to store thousands of documents, spreadsheets, and digital photos. You can upgrade to 100 gigabytes or more for a reasonable monthly fee. Files generated in Google applications don't count toward the account total.

If you are using a desktop or laptop PC or Mac, the Google Drive application can help you manage your files on your hard drive. This makes it easy to:

➤ Transfer files from your hard drive to Google Drive or download files from Google Drive, without using the browser interface.

➤ Keep backup copies of important files or folders.

➤ Work on files when you don't have an Internet connection.

The following pages explain how it all works.

How to install Google Drive on a PC or Mac

You will need to have a strong Internet connection to install the Google Drive desktop application.

1. Go to *http://drive.google.com*.

2. Select the Settings icon on the right side of the screen. Select the download option.

3. Choose the application to install. Backup & Sync is for personal files. Drive File Stream is for G Suite business accounts.

4. Download the installation file to your computer. Open it and follow the installation instructions.

5. Open the application. A login window will appear. Enter the email address and password associated with your Google Account.

6. Follow any additional instructions to complete the installation.

When you first install the Backup & Sync application, a new Google Drive folder will be installed on your hard drive, and selected files and folders associated with the account will be synced to the new folder (see image, below). Later, you can drag and drop new files into the Google Drive folder.

G Suite business accounts can use Drive File Stream, in which files are displayed as placeholders on the hard drive, and downloaded when selected or marked for offline access.

Version history in Google Drive

There's another fun feature of Google Drive that allows users to resurrect old versions of Google files. If you are the owner or editor of a shared document, you can revert to earlier versions of a document, even if other collaborators have made changes.

The *Version history* feature gets better: If you decide that you don't want to stick with the earlier version (or your collaborator demands that his version be brought back to life!) you can restore it. For Google files, you can revert to the earliest version of a document, spreadsheet or presentation, without any penalty or risk of deletion. (Version history is supported for certain non-Google formats, including Microsoft Office files, but only for 30 days.)

How to revert to an old version of a Google file

1. Open the document, spreadsheet or presentation.

2. Go to *File > Version history > See version history.*

3. The history will appear on the right side of the browser screen, with a list of all of the saved revisions and the people who made them (see screenshot, below).

4. Select an earlier version to view it onscreen.

5. Select *Restore this revision* to revert to that version.

6. To go back to the most recent version, bring up the revision history and find the version that you want to use (it should be near the top of the list).

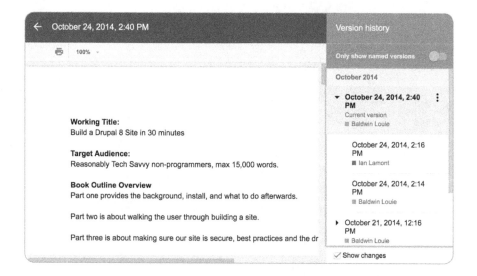

How to view an old version of a non-Google file

For non-Google formats (Microsoft Word, PDF, etc.), follow these steps to view older versions of the files:

1. Open Google Drive in Chrome or on a Chromebook.

2. Select the file, but don't open it.

3. Select the More Actions icon (three dots) and then select *Manage versions.*

4. Use the Manage Versions pop-up window to view and manage older versions of the files.

A personal message from the author, and a request

Thank you for purchasing the latest edition of *Google Drive & Docs In 30 Minutes!* Revising the guide was a huge challenge, not only because the online office suite has so many features, but also because Google is constantly improving it. Nevertheless, it was fun writing about Google's applications and providing clear, easy-to-understand instructions that will help you get the most out of the online office suite. If you have a question about Google Drive or the guide, please feel free to email me at *ian@in30minutes.com*.

I would also like to ask a favor. Could you take a minute to rate *Google Drive & Docs In 30 Minutes (2nd Edition)* and write a quick online review? An honest appraisal of the contents of *Google Drive & Docs In 30 Minutes* will not only be appreciated by me, but it will also let other potential readers know what to expect.

Thanks for reading!

Ian Lamont

P.S.: I have created "cheat sheets" for Google Drive, Docs, and Sheets, containing annotated lists of features, quick examples, and keyboard shortcuts. The four-panel references are printed on 8.5 by 11-inch high-quality card stock, perfect for desks, walls, and shelves. They also have holes for three-ring binders. Visit *in30minutes.com/cheatsheets* to learn more.

About the author

Google Drive & Docs In 30 Minutes is authored by Ian Lamont, an award-winning business and technology journalist and the founder of i30 Media Corporation. His media career has spanned more than 25 years across three continents, including a stint in the British music industry and a six-year residence in Taipei, where he learned Mandarin and worked for a local TV network and newspaper.

Lamont's writing and editorial work has garnered industry awards from the Society of American Business Editors and Writers (SABEW) and the American Society of Business Publication Editors (ASBPE). IN 30 MINUTES guides have received awards from the Independent Book Publishers Association and Foreword INDIES. His books include *Dropbox In 30 Minutes, Twitter In 30 Minutes,* and *Lean Media: How to focus creativity, streamline production, and create media that audiences love.*

Lamont is a graduate of the Boston University College of Communication and MIT's Sloan Fellows program. He lives with his family in the Boston area.

Keyboard shortcuts for Google Drive

Here is a list of basic shortcut keys for Google Drive, Docs, Sheets, Slides, and Drawings. All you need to do is type the keys in the list below to activate the corresponding commands. Why go through the trouble of remembering these shortcuts? You'll find typing them on your PC or laptop will save time compared to activating the same commands with a mouse. Note that while all of the listed shortcuts work in the Google Chrome browser, a few may not work in other browsers (Internet Explorer, Firefox, Safari, etc.).

Google Drive home screen

The following keyboard shortcuts work on Windows PCs, Macs, and Chromebooks.

c — Create new file

u — Upload new file

o — Open file

d — Information about file

j or **down arrow** — Advance to next file

k or **up arrow** — Go back to previous file

x — Select file

t — Open settings pane

n — Rename selected file

Other Google applications

Some of the keyboard shortcuts in Docs, Sheets, Forms, Slides, Drawings, and Sites, including commands used for copying and pasting text, are identical to those in Microsoft Office and other programs. Windows and Chrome OS (for Chromebooks) shortcuts are listed first, followed by their Mac equivalents.

Windows & Chrome OS

Control + / — Show all keyboard shortcuts

Control + ' — Go to next misspelling (Docs only)

Control + Shift + c — Word count (Docs only)

Control + o — Open file

Control + p — Print file

Control + f — Find text

Control + z — Undo

Control + y — Redo

Control + b — Bold text

Control + i — Italicize text

Control + u — Underline text

Control + a — Select all

Control + x — Cut selected text

Control + c — Copy selected text

Control + v — Paste

Control + k — Create link to web address

Alt + f — Open file menu

Alt + e — Open edit menu

Alt + v — Open view menu

Alt + i — Open insert menu

Alt + t — Open tools menu

Mac

Command + / — Show all keyboard shortcuts

Command + ' — Go to next misspelling (Docs only)

Command + Shift + c — Word count (Docs only)

Command + o — Open file

Command + p — Print file

Command + f — Find text

Command + z — Undo

Command + y — Redo

Command + b — Bold text

Command + i — Italicize text

Command + u — Underline text

Command + a — Select all

Command + x — Cut selected text

Command + c — Copy selected text

Command + v — Paste

Command + k — Create link to web address

Control + Option + f — Open file menu

Control + Option + e — Open edit menu

Control + Option + v — Open view menu

Control + Option + i — Open insert menu

Control + Option + t — Open tools menu

Index

Notes

CPSIA information can be obtained
at www.ICGtesting.com
Printed in the USA
LVHW04s0347270718
585048LV00014B/308/P

9 781939 924315